BETRAYED

Janine Harrington

Published in 2012 by FeedARead.com Publishing –
Arts Council funded

A CIP catalogue record for this title is available from
the British Library.

This is a true story.

This is my story.

The events portrayed are real.
Names and identifying features have been changed
to protect the innocent.
But the guilty are still out there …

Beware!

To Tony, who makes my life complete.
In doing so he gives me the courage, the wisdom,
the true 'happy-ever-after' experience
to write this book now

And in writing it,
I reach out to all those living in abuse
– mental, emotional, physical, sexual -
to illustrate through my own shared experience
you are not alone …

There is a life beyond.

I left you in April '78
to make a life of my own
I should have felt anger, I should have felt hate,
But all I cried for was Home.

You couldn't listen, you wouldn't try
To understand my point of view.
Shouting and swearing, you laughed when I cried
Until I said 'sorry' to you.

Remember the time you were watching TV
You'd knocked me out cold on the floor
I hadn't had time to make up your tea
And you couldn't wait any more.

And so I emptied the bottle of pills
That I'd had for depression and nerves.
But a knock at the door stopped me taking my fill,
Stopped me doing what I thought I deserved.

The doctor was patient, he put up a show,
Prescribing pills if I got worse.
He said given time my depression would go,
That is, if I didn't first!

That was the moment I made up my mind,
Knew exactly what I had to do.
I packed my possessions, well, those I could find,
And left my past life and you.

There was no quarrel, there was no row,
No empty words, I just went.
The blood and the bruises don't matter now
Just all those wasted years spent.

© Janine Harrington

Colour Me Green

'I used to believe I was a good girl
But then, if I am a good girl
Why do all these good people
Want to hurt me?'

Green.

Everywhere I look there is Green. The colour makes me sick, hurt, afraid. I close my eyes, trying to block out the Green, hiding behind my lids. But the colour won't go away. It holds me, wrapping itself around me, not letting me go. Forcing me to become a part of itself. Taking away my identity and the person I am now. And all the time it's squeezing my tummy into knots, filling pockets with dread, champing and gnawing on all the tender bits, reminding me just how bad it feels.

'Mummy?'

I'm not sure the words leave my lips. But Mummy is there. Mummy will know. Mummy will make it better. I reach out a hand. Try to make contact. Needing to feel special, loved. To know that Mummy understands. But there is just the cold wood of the bench on which we sit. Mummy is turned away, talking with someone. I feel alone. Abandoned. Swallowed up by Green. Green is the enemy. It *wants* me to feel bad. That's what it's there for. It is coming to get me. It is going to eat me all

6

up and make me disappear and then nothing will ever be quite the same again.

*　　*　　*　　*

'Come on, now. It isn't that bad.'

They're trying to trick me. To make me think it's something else ....

'The sooner you come in the sooner it will be over.'

That's always a sign something is going to happen. Something very bad!

'Come on, Cherub. Mummy's here. Hold my hand. It will be all right.'

My hands still hurt from being prised away from the green of the railings outside. I was screaming then, begging them not to take me in. I'd tried to tell them ... to say what would happen. But I couldn't find words they could understand. Sometimes there aren't words for what you feel inside. I wanted to go home like I want to go home now. But the more I say it ... *scream it ... shout it ...* the more they want to take me in. My feelings don't matter at all. The cold metal railings offered comfort, hope, strength ... for a while. As long as I held on, I was safe.

But then the green railings deceived me. They let me go.

'Come on, don't be a silly girl. After, we'll go and have a treat in the café and a ride on the donkeys. But you have to be a good girl first. D'you hear?'

Yes! I hear. Yes! I want the treat in the café. Yes! I want to go on the donkeys. Of course I do ... yes, yes, yes. But no! I won't go inside. Treats always come after something very very bad.

'Nobody's going to hurt you.'

It feels like a slap. They aren't listening to me. Or maybe they don't understand. All my crying and screaming and shouting has been for nothing. In the end, they have forced my fingers from their grip on the railings one by one by one. Carrying me in, placing me on the bench where I sit now. They've done it a hundred times before. And I'm just as powerless as I have always been.

Green is in control.

Green.

Green is everywhere I look. So much space. So much Green. It swirls under my feet on the tiled floor, catching in the cracks between, menacing, threatening, drawing me in. It is painted thick on the walls. Even the doors are Green. It is closing tight around my world.

* * * *

A door opens. A white figure steps through. My tummy lurches into a new kind of panic. Silently, I scream. My fingers open and close without anything to hang on to, as if trying to speak for me. One figure is followed by another. A wheelchair squeals in protest. The door closes. But before I can let out my breath, another door opens, this time further along. Matron begins reading from a list of names. Teacups rattle in saucers. Voices clammer, confusing the sound of the words. Children jump up and down, running wildly in and around the chairs while parents shout after them.

A name is shouted again across the crowded hall. A mother and child stand up amidst the confusion to follow her inside. The door closes behind them. Green swallows them up until they are no more.

Green.

It reminds me of something ... and before I can remember the memory is snatched away. It isn't a nice warm feeling. It doesn't make me happy inside. My tummy jumps and aches as if it's alive. Each time a name is called it brings fresh panic until I'm almost wetting the seat with dread. I squirm on the bench, placing a hand to the front of my blue dungarees, wondering that I don't see the pain when I look down it feels so bad. It's the same feeling I have when I'm taken to the dentist ... only worse ... ten, a hundred, a zillion times worse!

Green is too close. Too threatening. I reach for Rosemary at my side and sit the doll on my lap, holding her instead. I curl a finger inside her sculpted hand, encouraging the doll to see for me, trying to bring magic back into my world.

* * * *

An old man clomps towards me. He leans heavily, a wooden crutch resting under one arm.

Is that what they do to you if you are bad? If you don't do what they say?

I cringe away, trying to become part of the wall, staring hard at the ground. One of his trouser legs is empty, pinned beneath him. One leg falls to the floor in step with the stick. I listen to the steady *step clunk ... step clunk ... step clunk ...* until he is out of sight. A nurse bustles past. Her uniform crackles. The tray she is carrying tinkles its metal instruments in tune.

Matron is calling a name ... It is my name. My time has come.

'*Janine Harrington ... Janine Harrington ...* '

I try making my small frame even smaller, crouching in a quivering heap on the hard wooden bench. Mummy is alert, active, ready, trying to haul me into a sitting position. I slither down further, trying to hide out of sight.

'Take your boots off, there's a good girl. Socks and boots ... so you're ready for Doctor ... listen ... your name is being called now. Be a good girl now ...'

Right on cue, the starched voice rings once more across the hall.

'*Janine Harrington ... Janine ...* Ah! There you are ... come on, come on, dear, Doctor is waiting ... we can't keep Doctor waiting, you know. He's an important man.'

Matron strides into action, feet clacking on the green and cream tiled floor, taking charge of the recalcitrant child dragging on her arm.

'Come on … come ON! We have this every time … every time you cause a delay. Doctor is far too busy for this kind of nonsense …'

'Mummy … *Muuuuu … mmy*?'

'Now come on, you're a big girl. Four years old. We'll leave Mummy here to rest, she's not feeling very well. You're going to be having a baby sister soon then you'll have someone to play with. Won't that be nice? Now come with me dear and I'll take you in to see Doctor.'

'*Mummy*?'

Choked tears. The crisp starched uniform offers no comfort. She has firm hold of my arm. I clutch my fawn coloured socks dragged from my feet in one hand, Rosemary clasped firm in the other. The pair of weighty callipers has already been lifted from me. And then, as if I need a reminder, a man hobbles towards me on crutches. It is his right leg. *Same as mine*! My leg twitches in sympathy. I wonder what he did to make it happen? What did he do that was so bad? Or maybe he had a secret like mine he shared? We exchange hooded glances before I look down hurriedly, my small bare left foot tripping over the right. The same kind of punishment could be easily metered out to me.

11

Green.

Green stands waiting for me to enter. It beckons me in.

* * * *

The Doctor is sitting just as if he's never moved from last time I saw him. His swivel chair tilts forward. The door opens wider. Matron hauls me through.

I sit as instructed on the cork bench in front of the swivelly specialist's chair. The desk looks huge. Everything looks big and threatening. And I still can't feel anything except an overwhelming sickening dread. The face of the Doctor is hidden behind papers … is it the good one?

Is it the bad?

He turns to face me … *and I know*!

'Ah … Rosemary … now you're going to be a *good girl*, aren't you? A *good girl*, mind!'

I bend Rosemary's legs to sit comfortably on the stool beside me. She has on her warm woollen green outfit specially knitted by Mummy. I keep my eyes averted from the long faded green curtains behind which hides the black leather couch.

I'm used to the Doctor talking to me through my doll.

'Lift your leg up for me … that's it … Matron, thank you, that's all for now. I'll call you if I need you.'

'Yes, Doctor.'

My world collapses around me. My mind numbs. I can't think, can't feel, can't speak, can't … My face is frozen. He's speaking carefully to my doll and our selves merge.

But then … there are no more words.

Silence.

Dread gnaws the insides of my stomach. The six pairs of knickers I am wearing are leaking. I pull protectively at my dungarees … but it's no use. He's finished prodding and poking my malformed right foot already turned inwards, back to its preferred state. He is nodding towards the curtains, eyebrows raised and quizzical, daring me to disobey. His eyes penetrate the wall I have built around myself. They dry my mouth. Water my eyes. Shake my body, my legs, my arms and hands. I don't want to belong to this body any more … I don't want to be me … I don't even want to be here … I'm not here really …

I'm the invisible child.

On automatic pilot, Rosemary straightens her knees. Together, reluctant, we pull the curtain apart. I look back. He is watching. His hands motion us on, impatient. Best to get it over and done with … and be away … away from this man, this room, the hospital and all it stands for …

Green curtains close around me. Green becomes my world … enveloping .. swamping … drawing me in.

Green.

Green has finally swallowed me up. Now I am locked into Green I know I can't get away.

Mechanically, with a mind of their own, my hands remove my dungarees. The large black couch rubs as I climb on top. It feels shiny and smooth and squeaky clean. I sit waiting, holding my dungarees close, clutching my doll at my side. Gazing interminably into the Green of the curtains that surround me.

* * * *

When hands finally grasp the curtains, pulling them violently apart, I jump. All I can see is the white coat. All I can feel are the hands pushing me down, his back towards me, shielding what might happen next. All I know for certain is that my jumper is dragged up. My pants pulled down – all six pairs of them. My legs part reluctantly. And the probing and prodding begins. I feel the measure stick at the side of one leg and then the other. And then, like spiders creeping up the insides of my body, fingers begin their ascent.

Little Miss Muffet sat on a tuffet
Eating her curds and whey …

I don't have that pinafore dress on today with little Miss Muffet embroidered on the front. Trousers are safer. And extra pairs of pants I have on shielding my body from hurt.

But it happens anyway.

All I can see is the back of his white coat as he turns away from me, blocking my view. Unseen hands continue to stroke my legs … stretching … measuring one against the other with the long round tapered rule. It's a race the smaller thinner right leg can never win. It's asking the impossible. More than five inches shorter than the other … the foot with no ankle, turned ninety degrees inwards. It has no chance of ever being 'normal'. Sometimes grown-ups can be so stupid! But I'm just a child, what do I know? I'm the guinea pig they're testing new theories out on.

> *There came a big spider*
> *Who sat down beside her*
> *And frightened Miss Muffet away.*

The spider enters my secret place. Fingers probe my private cave. Prising lips apart. Going even where my own fingers aren't allowed. I want to pee, but I can't make a mess. Besides, he will see. That wouldn't be nice, not what a good girl might do.

Rosemary, my doll, looks on.

Only the Green exists now.

Only the Green.

Green.

Green equals itching, aching, burning, hurting. Pain and sensation I don't understand and can never explain. Green is all that matters now. My eyes stare at the dark olive green curtain surrounding the couch on all sides, while the Specialist with his back turned towards me, carries on the hurt with his hands.

Green.

Green has taken control.

Colour Me White

*Child is being able to keep hold of the Dream
and to live as if it were today*

Right from the beginning I could never make sense of my life. Always, it was a giant jigsaw, with so many pieces missing I was never going to make sense of the whole.

The main picture for the puzzle was a map of unchartered territory. As each day drew to a close, wistfully I placed a piece of puzzle in position, looking back the way I had come. I knew there were places I had been before and yet could not remember. They became blanks in my mind. Like a half-forgotten melody, I caught the smallest of sound and images in their passing … but then … then … then they were gone. I couldn't hold on to them for long. In the end, it was hard to know what was real and how much imagined. The more I questioned the more confusing the outcome.

'You had a happy childhood … the happiest … you were a happy smiling little girl … always. Look at the photographs. Oh you were such a good sweet girl … always doing what you were told.'

Photos don't lie … do they?

There isn't one photograph of me wearing callipers.

Certainly there are no photographs of the hospital. It was never talked about, neither was my disability. We just landed there … then we were home. I had absolutely no memory of what had taken place by the time I was playing with Charlie at the bottom of the garden. As my sister was born and grew up, and then another sister, both believed I was special, treated different by our parents, taken off on mystery trips every few days, arriving home talking about rides on donkeys and cake in the café.

Deception? The misguided belief that they were in some way protecting, retaining an innocence already taken?

Somewhere deep inside me was the truth. It couldn't be denied forever. It was just that the truth was hard to cope with, to accept anything other than a normal happy childhood had happened … to me.

What made it all the harder was that no-one answered questions or took the trouble to explain. And because I was a small child, my fears remained larger than life, haunting my waking and sleeping moments, giving me nightmares, leaving me on edge, cramping my stomach into knots with a dread I couldn't explain … because I couldn't remember.

And one more thing … nothing was what it seemed.

Home was a castle. A chair was a cave. Sheets hanging on the line were tents for the Indians. Wooden slats created wigwams. A wooden box was much more exciting than what came in it because it was a ship, a galleon, in which I could sail the seas, reaching for land, taking on whatever life I chose. I lived in a storybook fantasy world of illusion.

It is my mother's diaries which hold unexpected clues giving memory clarity and form:

4ᵗʰ July 1953

Janine is born after a long hard labour. It is a painful birth. There is the physical manipulation of turning baby around to her right position, and then she is twenty minutes in the birth canal, the maximum time.

Baby Janine turns blue during feeds and is placed in an oxygen tent. Days later it is discovered she has 'talipes equinovarus', a 'club' foot ...

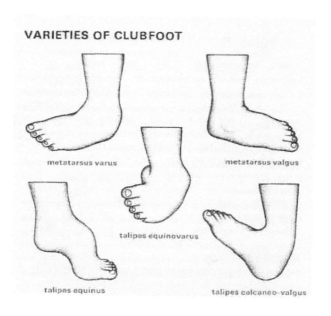

VARIETIES OF CLUBFOOT

metatarsus varus

metatarsus valgus

talipes equinovarus

talipes equinus

talipes calcaneo-valgus

It means a malformation and turning inwards of the right foot, and shortening andthinning of the leg. She cries a lot and has to be dosed at night. Her feet are barred together with a splint.

12th November 1953

Mr Robinson, a Specialist at the hospital; puts splints on each leg with an iron bar between. It needs a spanner to enable a proper bath! Janine has hysterics at having her legs tied together in this way. But with the iron bar removed, it means she hurts herself with the protruding ends. There is a lot of pain from her foot. She has to be dosed at night regularly.

The Drs are experimenting with treatment.

1954

We are seeing Mr Robinson's assistant, another Specialist. Janine displays uncontrollable sobbing at hospital and at home. She is also having nightmares.

5th June 1956

We are visiting the Orthopaedic Hospital three times a week to see a Specialist and to collect special boots (calipers) to wear. I try to insist we see Mr Robinson only, because of Janine's apparent terror at seeing the other Specialist. Besides, both are offering completely different treatments!

Today, I was rather shaken to find Janine on one side of the fence in our garden and Charlie on the other side. She says they are playing 'Doctors and Patients'. Not doctors and nurses? On investigation, find that she has no pants on and is lying down ...

I just do not feel Janine is safe. She remains locked up in her own back garden by herself for her own good. She is still uncontrollably sobbing and continues to sleep with us most nights.

9th October 1956
Janine wants to know where Heaven is and whether Mummy and Daddy can all go to Jesus together with her. Please God – yes!

24th January 1957
Hospital with Janine to have plaster removed and to collect new boots. Her resistance to doctors starts as soon as we approach the hospital. 'Ham-handed' male nurse in plaster room using a sawing machine to cut the plaster off cuts through her leg, making it bleed, leaving the leg very sore and tender, but she walks back to the bus stop in her new calliper boots.

5th April 1957
We continue with hospital visits three times a week. Janine's right foot is often in plaster to force it into position.

There have been further episodes of 'Drs and Patients' *with Charlie next door at the bottom of the garden. I could murder anyone who tries to sully her! Charlie's mum has warned that Janine and Charlie are not safe to be left alone together. But more episodes follow.*

20th June 1957
Hospital. See Greek doctor who recommends plaster treatment instead of boots. This means attending hospital every week for nine months to have plaster notched and adjusted.

27th June 1957

Hospital to have plaster notched and redone. Janine has a restless night sobbing and kicking out in her sleep. I think the sawing of the plaster frightens her, especially as she has been cut and damaged by this and she relives it in her sleep.

4th July 1957

Janine's birthday – four years old today!
Hospital for 9am to have her plaster notched. Janine holds tightly to me and Dolly and blames Rosemary for crying!!!

9th July 1957

Janine is very thrilled with her Dolly Nanny gave her for her birthday. She says:
"This is the very special doll I wanted. Did Nanny see her floating on a pink-tipped cloud and get her for me? That's how she was borned, wasn't it, Mummy? Now she's my little girl like I am yours. I've got to take care of her and protect her."
Janine puts Dolly to bed and sings her own brand of calypso, like Daddy did to her last night. Janine asks for Dolly to be christened 'Rosemary', so, in as reverent a way as I can, I pretend to be Rev Jeeves and christen her 'Rosemary' while Janine solemnly makes her promises.

1957

Continue to attend hospital for notching of plasters once a week. Uncontrollable sobbing from Janine continues with each visit – clingy, wanting Mummy all the time. Dreaming badly, sleeps with Mummy and Daddy.

1957

Janine continuously wakes screaming at night.
Tantrums in day. Uncontrollable sobbing. Put it
down to 'ridding herself of surplus emotion'.

All the time she seems to need extra comfort,
extra love, surrounding herself with dolls. Charlie
(one year older, his birthday day after Janine) and
her are inseparable.

1st August 1957

Demand to see Mr Robinson (only through kindness
of Red Cross Nurse is my demand adhered to). He
promptly orders plaster off and binds leg with
surgical bandage. Foot shows mark of being
pinched during notching. Says to see him next week.
Leg is very thin, foot very puffy, skin very raw.

8th August 1957

Hospital. Mr Robinson says to continue with the
boots and night splint and to stretch leg as much as
possible. Says to see him again in a month.

17th November 1957

Janine sleeps surrounded by all her dolls so that
there is hardly room for herself – Rosemary, June,
Rosebud .. This perhaps denotes a need for comfort
and extra love. I don't know why.

19th November 1957

Hospital. See Mr Robinson (but have to dodge to
keep out of Greek doctor's way), and Janine is
measured for another pair of boots. Janine asks for
first time when she can stop going to the hospital,
when she can stop wearing 'those boots' - ? I wish I
knew.

29th May 1958
Baby sister born.

Colour Me Blind

*The walls that we build for protection
so easily can become our prison*

Three times a week we visit the hospital. Always it's the same. Sometimes I go home in plaster. Sometimes I need fitting for a new pair of brown leather lace up boots where the iron bar slots into the heel, reaching up my leg to buckle at the knee.

Once home, it's *'Doctors and Patients'* I want to play with Charlie, somehow trying to work it through in my mind, to remember, to understand, to find words for the unexplained. And then of course there is Stripy, my imaginary friend … passengers have to make room for him on the bus, a chair has to be set at table, always there is room in my bed. I break out into screaming fits if it isn't so. Stripy the tiger is a valued part of my life … the only form of protection I have.

One day Mummy is packing a small bag.

'What are you doing that for? Where are we going? Why aren't you and Daddy packing a bag too?'

'You'll see … now, go get that new nightie we bought the other day …'

It's a long bus ride away. But then … a familiar line of long narrow pointed green railings inch up the hill to a building at the top …

Hospital!

Landmarks are achingly familiar. I dread what comes next. Just as always, I cling onto the green railings outside until the orderly comes to prise me away, across the green and cream tiled floor to the waiting room, the hard wooden seats …

And Matron.

But this time it's different. This time it's a different entrance we pass through. It's a different waiting room, smaller, a different part of the hospital. There are beds, and children in nightwear sitting empty eyed in silence.

'Mummy …?'

'Now Cherub, you've got to be a very brave little girl … You can do that for Mummy, can't you?'

'Thank you, Mrs Harrington. We'll take it from here. It's best … you can visit later …'

'Mummy …?'

Mummy turns to leave. I turn my head into the pillow and weep in the arms of my doll. Rosemary, with clear blue eyes wide open, stares accusingly at the departing figure, slipping away into another world and the safeness of Home.

'Get undressed, there's a good girl. You'll need to put your nightie on before Doctor comes round ...'

Doctor? Nightie? Undressed?

It's a trap ... another way to get me just the way they want me. I didn't see it coming. But what could I do? They have the power. They are in control.

* * * *

They come, figures in white. Hands force me into a back-to-front gown. It takes two of them to give me the injection which should make me sleep ... screaming into pillows, balling my hands into fists trying to fight off the enemy ... they turn me over, pushing the needle in my cheek. Curtains close around me. I am alone. Rosemary furrows into my arms as I try to close off my mind, lulled by the radio playing as the rest of the children leave the ward for their midday snack:

> *"I have come to the end of my lollipop,*
> *To the end, to the end of my lollipop.*
> *I have come to the end of my lollipop,*
> *Plop goes my heart."*

Lollipops. Sitting in the garden with Charlie. Charlie will be waiting for me. Wondering where I am. We are always together. Reaching through the wooden fence that divides our gardens.

I've tried to sort it in my mind through play. To say it in the only way I know. Just like any normal child would. Almost from the moment I was born I knew I was different. But Charlie knows. Charlie is safe. He

27

takes all the bad feelings away. He makes me feel
Normal and happy … a good girl.

Sleep doesn't come. But then, I don't want it to. I
want to go on thinking about Charlie, playing with him
in my mind, to make the bad things go away.

Just like in the cubicle with the Specialist, I don't
want to think about what might happen next. Because
somehow, no matter how many times I do as I'm told,
they always want more. And in trying to understand
that, I've talked to Mummy, tried to say how much it
hurts. How much HE hurts. But that was wrong. It's the
reason I've ended up here … to be punished.

*I'm being punished for telling my secret … and it
isn't going to go away … ever!*

Faces peer around the curtain. It isn't going
according to plan. I'm not asleep. I sense their
frustration. But they can't make me. They'll just have
to send me home. I hear their hurried whispers,
wondering what to do. I wish they would hurry up and
call Mummy to come take me away.

A trolley appears. A memory stirs.

'I want my Mummy,' I demand, in a small clear
voice so that there can be no mistake about my need.
The wheels squeal in protest down the corridor under
glaring lights, carrying me into other corridors, other
rooms.

'I want my Mummy NOW!'

I gaze upwards, defiant into the face of the nurse above me, pushing me along.

'Mummy … where's my Mummy?'

'Mummy is here. I'm here. Everything will be all right. Shush now, try to sleep.'

'Mummy?'

I'm not even woozy. And I'm definitely not dreaming. So they're tricking me. This is some new game which they want me to play. And I don't know the rules. So what's new? Now they want me to believe something that just isn't true … that nurse is Mummy? I watch the lips of the nurse move in time with the words:

'It's all right. Really it is, Pet. Just you settle down and go to sleep … there's a good girl.'

Those words. '*Good girl*'. But she isn't Mummy, no matter how much she pretends. Mummy doesn't call me '*Pet*'. She calls me '*Cherub*'. Is she pretending to be Mummy? She's an adult. Adults don't tell lies.

Mummy? My Mummy? She couldn't be … *could she*? Or then again, maybe she is. Maybe she is my Mummy now. I am being punished, after all.

'Ups-a-daisy. Over we go.'

I am lifted from trolley onto bed. And immediately I'm struggling, a trapped frightened bird eager to be free.

'I'm sorry, Doctor. We couldn't get her to sleep.'

I see Green pushing its way through … restricting … trapping … tainting my world as only Green can. Green … Green coming to take control.

He can't be here as well … the Specialist? … prodding, poking, prising, pushing, hurting …?

My tummy lurches in recognition, flapping like a cluster of butterflies on a summer's day. A silly cap covers his head. A mask covers his face. They are in disguise. They want to confuse me so I won't tell.

Masked faces peer down at me from all sides, tutting, shaking their covered heads. Lights flash crazily in my eyes, bright and white and dazzling. But below, I can see they are wearing wellies … green wellies. Their gowns are green, their masks, now their wellies … a part of Green … a part of the pain … a part of the nightmare that makes up my world.

'*NOOOOooooo!* Let me *GOOOOOooooo!*'

They smother my cries. I feel a hurting pressure in my bottom. *Is this a new kind of torture? Will they force me first to feel the confusion of sensation before they start to tear at my limbs*? I feel for the doll at my side. Rosemary isn't there! So they've taken my doll as well!

Green.

Green closing in … merging now with grey … with black … with a long dark crazy tunnel of nothingness.

* * * *

I open my eyes to see the curtains once more circling my bed. It hasn't really happened. It's all been just a bad bad dream. A nightmare. Like the many I have at home. Or else it happened to someone else. But I can still see the pain. A living thing. Squirming in the Green. I feel for Rosemary at my side. She is there. I snuggle into her. Comforting. All-seeing. All-knowing. My Friend.

* * * *

Again, I wake. This time the curtains are gone. The girl across the way waves, welcoming me back. I struggle to sit up. I can't wave lying down. And it is then I see for the first time the hump rising at the foot of my bed. I can't break free. Somehow it's holding me down. I seem somehow attached to the hump. I try to pull away. It hurts. I try again, more gently, exploring its boundaries. It feels like a cage erected to my bed to hold me in place.

To stop me escaping?

As I search for a meaning to the hump, I remember the *step clump ... step clump ... step clump ...* The man walking with the aid of a crutch up and down, down and up, up and down the corridors of the hospital. The voices. The hands holding me down. The nurse saying she is '*Mummy*'. Needles forcing me to sleep under their control.

I know then they have taken my leg as punishment, for trying to tell Mummy what they are doing to me.

31

A scream starts from a long way off. It spreads closer and closer, louder and louder and louder.

It is coming from the very depths of my soul.

* * * *

4th July 1958

Janine's birthday – five years old! Dress-up birthday party with Charlie, Stan and friends in the garden.

6th July 1958

Introduce the subject of hospitals to Janine prior to her going in on Tuesday for an operation. Try to make it sound like a game, but nothing can disguise the piteous 'cis du coeur' at bedtime: 'Mummy, I don't want to go to hospital'. If only I could wave a magic wand!

7th July 1958

Again: Mummy, I don't want to go into hospital'. Janine cries. Sing her to sleep with 'It's a sin to tell a lie ...'

8th July 1958

Take Janine to hospital with Rosemary. Janine sits on my lap and cries all the way there. At the final parting, she clings to my skirts and screams: 'Mummy, don't let them take me away. I want to stay with you'. The Sister has to tear her from my side. Later, I peep at her – she is sitting in her dressing gown staring out the windows with dull lifeless eyes, like a wild bird of the sky that has been caught and caged. Oh my Janine!

9th July 1958

Visit Janine at hospital. She looks dreadful – very pale and trembling from head to foot so that I have to hold her glass of orange juice. She also complains of pains in her chest and is very weepy. Jack and I feel very depressed.

10th July 1958

Bring Janine home from hospital. Daddy has a surprise for her - a Doctor Outfit (complete with a real working stethoscope).

11th July 1958

Janine sobbing uncontrollably. Nightmares!

2nd September 1958

Janine starts school. I believe contact with the outside world is influencing Janine too much. She is becoming too questioning, too demanding in wanting Mummy to listen to HER needs and what it is SHE wants to do.

1959

Hospital visits continue weekly.

Find Janine at the bottom fo the garden again with Charlie. They say they are playing 'Doctors and Patients'. Upset. Pledge between Janine and Charlie to marry. Janine's Protector? Jack is out most evenings. I (Mummy) is constant. She continues to sleep with us, plagued by nightmares.

1959

Charlie's influence, filling her head, thoughts of getting married to him. Like fairy tale endings, she says: '... and they live happy ever after ... no more hurt.' Sometimes it's as though her head is big enough to hold only one person at a time. Usually it is me. Mummy. Now it is Charlie. Only him.

18th June 1960
A second sister is born.

25th April 1961
Hospital with Janine for admission for operation. Same Sister as before. German wardress type, glazed white front, impeccable – snatches Janine into custody! Returns her briefly, clad in dressing-gown and slippers for last farewell kiss, and escorts her to balcony for last wave – all against Matron's wishes.

27th April 1961
Visit Janine in hospital 6.30-7pm. Very trembly and shaky and weepy. Palms of hands burning hot and I blow on them to cool them down. May come home Sunday if temperature drops. Not a happy ward she is in ...

10th May 1961
Jack visits Janine in hospital. Learning to walk on crutches.

12th May 1961
Hospital to bring Janine home – to stay off leg for three weeks.

22nd June 1961
Hospital with Janine to have plaster removed. Wait two hours to see coloured Doctor ... Janine screams out of all proportion ...

Colour Me Blue

We live from inside out

In a detached bungalow on the side of a hill, situated in a quiet cul-de-sac on the outskirts of London where my father worked, I lived as an auburn haired child, lost in my imagination, in a place deep inside my head. It was my world. I could have all manner of witches, giants, dragons and beasties because I had the power to eliminate as well as to create ... it was a world of my own making. I was in control, with the power to make anything happen, to make everything go away. No-one ever really got hurt. It was all just make-believe.

Within the boundary of my world was a garden at the back of the bungalow reached through an archway of roses, my father's pride and joy. At the very bottom, by the hole in the hedge, my secret place; strawberries, raspberries, blackcurrants and gooseberries grew in abundance. While close to the back door, surrounded by a rockery, was a pool in which lilies floated and goldfish played.

On a Saturday morning, I would walk with Daddy down the hill, through the alleyway, and up into the high street to the library. Assistants all knew me and would exchange glances as I peeked up over the very high counter to have my books stamped in and out. I assured them one day they would look to find my own name on the spine of a book ... one day I would become a writer, an author, and write stories of my own. They would smile sympathetically and watch me trip awkwardly, one foot over the other, in my cumbersome boots, then dragging my right behind me in going out the door. I wasn't ever going to have a real life - be able to drive, go to work, do things without assistance – never mind the extraordinary like have a vocation or career.

Having taught me to read and write early, Mummy tried to keep me home, to teach me there rather than let me go to school where she was afraid I would be jeered at and teased. She wanted to keep me apart from the outside world, to protect and keep me safe. She carried her own guilt, believing in the sins of the forefathers and the mistaken belief that somehow she was responsible for my disability in a past life. Perhaps that is why it was never acknowledged, never spoken about, my questions never answered. It was easier to believe it didn't exist at all. But then, just after my first operation, with a leg in plaster, still haunted by what was happening to me; she presented me in a pushchair at the school gates. The teacher wondered, especially when it came to P.E, why I had on six pairs of knickers! I couldn't explain why. I didn't know. By then it was a reflex action when entering the outside world ... *just in case.* Just in case what? I didn't have the words to explain.

Daddy left at six every weekday morning to catch his train for work in the City. Just like going to hospital, it was always Mummy who took me to school. Gradually, we set up a routine where we'd play peep-bo either side of the hedge and made a game of it just so I would get there. I was never sure what days I would end up at hospital, and which days school. *Hospital ... school ... school ... hospital ...* I'd dither in the bathroom, retreating to a place deep within myself, tracing a finger round the white tiles, as if tracking my journey of life on the edge of a reality I didn't understand, dressed always for the worst. Like prising me off the green railings of the hospital, I'd need to be prised away from home, always late, never knowing where I was really going until I arrived.

Weekends, we'd pack a picnic and walk in the cornfields behind the barracks where summers lasted a lifetime. And in winter, we had snowball fights in the garden and made snowmen.

Christmas and birthdays were magic. I'd wake to '*Happy Birthday*' or '*Happy Christmas*' being sung at my bedside, heaps of hugs, kisses and surprises. One main present and lots of little ones was always the rule at Christmas with the little fir tree dug from the garden for the occasion. While birthdays meant a party and selected friends from school in fancy dress so that we could easily escape into whichever world I wanted to write about and explore at the time.

At bedtime there were always prayers, kneeling at the side of my bed, where I laid out my concerns of the day, and asked God to bless every one of my family and friends, a list of all the people I knew. *Did I pray for the Specialist? Did I even remember him? Probably not!* It was a question asked in therapy in later years, by a Christian counsellor, who pronounced the reason I could not get over the effects of my past was due to the fact I had never forgiven him.

On either side of our bungalow lived Charlie and Stan, my extended family, my brothers. Stan was a slow, methodical boy, always trying to catch up, to understand the games we played. His mother was the hairdresser who cut my hair. His father let off fireworks in November, pushing the family Alsatian indoors out of harm's way, while Catherine wheels and rockets exploded, lighting up the night sky, filling it with a sense of wonder. He built us a wooden tree house, where we'd sit and look out at our world. But it was with Charlie that we explored faraway imaginary places, entering into a world that was uniquely ours, filled with excitement and adventure. An old upturned chair became an Aladdin's cave. Planks of wood tilted one against the other became a wigwam, and with feathers collected from the birds in my hair, we'd mount war one against the other ... Charlie the cowboy with his treasured cap gun, me Hiawatha, so often taken captive and tied up at a stake until parents called us in for tea. Another day I would be Maid Marion and he Robin Hood with imaginary merry men, armed with arrows capped with plastic stickers, outlaws, foraging for food, finding shelter in amongst the foliage in the confines of my garden.

Charlie was my knight in shining armour ... always. He understood me as no-one else could. I'd watch in awe as he went down on bended knee in front of Mummy, begging her to let me remove my calliper boots for *'just one day'* so I could be Normal. We were already promised to one another. I knew one day we would marry. One day he would carry me away to live forever in our own private, unique and very special world. With Charlie I could be whoever I wanted, and there were always so many new and wonderful places to discover together. We were more than friends. We were 'brother' and 'sister' ... comrades in arms ... confidantes ... soulmates. Through his eyes he saw the world in the same way as I. Every day we turned a fresh page and found new things to capture and explore within our imagination. Nothing stayed the same. And when it was time for Charlie to go home, it was as if he took something of myself away with him – something precious, something almost sacred. Away from Charlie I was an only lonely child who created imaginary friends to fill an aching void.

But then completely without warning, my life shifted and changed forever in a way not even I could imagine.

Colour Me Grey

*Fear holds us back from enjoying
the Freedom that is ours*

Huge wooden chests start to appear in the hall. *Where did they come from? Who put them there? What are they to be used for? What's going on?*

'What are these for, Mummy?'

'Oh, you'll see, Cherub. You'll see ... now run along and play.'

Always the same ... I'm well used to it now. Questions left hanging. But then, coming in from the garden on a beautiful summer day in search of something to quench my thirst, I see the chests are filling with newspaper-wrapped items. Mummy is opening and closing cupboards, wrapping everyday things, stacking them into the boxes like it's her life's mission.

I've been lying on a mattress at the far end of the garden. My books are still out there, gateways to other lands. I have struggled for a while to break away, caught in the grip of a mystery ... the Famous Five are following clues. I need to go back and join them, see where the trail might lead. But curiosity kicks in. There could be an adventure right here!

'Mummy?'

'Yes, Cherub.'

'We're going to be needing those things you're packing away. We still use them, don't we? Are we getting rid of them? All of them? All our belongings? Why? Don't we need them any more? Are we getting new things? And which things of mine will have to go?'

Mummy laughs, but her hands are never still, frenziedly reaching for another pot or jar or container, plucking a fresh sheet of newspaper, placing an item in the centre and wrapping the newsprint tight around it.

It occurs to me Daddy hasn't been around. The routine has changed. He's been away for days. Suddenly, he returns unexpectedly and our life is being packed into boxes ... for why?

'You can help if you like.'

'Is it a new game, Mummy?'

'Yes, Cherub. Yes, it is a new game ... something we haven't tried before. This is how it works. We wrap each item I put on the table nice and tight in newspaper ... like this ... that's right. Just copy how I'm doing it. Good girl!'

I'm learning fast. Maybe if I stay and see this through the answers I seek will come. Daddy remains behind the closed door of a room at the back of the bungalow. '*Do not disturb.*' For a couple of hours maybe we continue filling one chest, then two. But I'm still curious. And as if to waylay further questions:

'Let's take a break, have some lunch. Daddy will be hungry. We can switch on the wireless for '*Listen with Mother*' and '*Woman's Hour*' ... and then do some more.'

'*Listen with Mother*', broadcast by the Home Service, is for children aged five and under. I am nine years old. My two sisters are just two and four.

"*Are you sitting comfortably? Then I'll begin ...*"

The broadcast begins. My sisters snuggle up alongside, listening intently to the story. But my own thoughts are racing. *Why isn't Daddy at work? What do the crates mean?* In many ways, they become symbolic of my callipers. No-one speaks about them. And yet they are here ... or are they? Could they be a figment of my imagination?

'P'raps they're having a clear out,' Charlie suggests helpfully.

'P'raps,' I'm not convinced. Something strange is going on, something important. I follow my parents around, making notes on their movements just as Fatty does in *The Secret Seven*.

But then, Slim's pick-up truck from further down the hill pulls up outside our front door. I've never really paid any attention to it before. It's always parked up, or gone, and then back again. Nothing to do with my world. Now all my thoughts are focused on it.

Crates are loaded on to the back, while my sisters and I are bundled into the front cab, with Mummy squashed in at our side, the youngest on her lap.

'Right girls, this is The Big Adventure!'

The truck slips away. I watch the road ahead, searching for clues. But soon, I am lost, the journey is long, my eyes close like my sisters at my side. Mummy and the driver talk in whispers until everything laps into silence.

Then ...

'Come on, girls ... we've arrived!'

Arrived? Arrived where? For how long?

The house is big and old and cold and damp. There's no heating except for an open fire. A tin bath is propped against the wall. But there are stairs, now there's a novelty! And it has an outside loo. It takes courage to creep out into the dark at night, down the long acreage of garden. My two sisters are scared so I need to be shaken awake to go with them. In the morning, we discover an orchard beyond where children come scrumping. And suddenly there is a whole new land just waiting to be explored. But oh how I miss the pond. I worry about the goldfish needing feeding. We'd brought some of the raspberries and strawberries we'd been picking, but what about the rest? As the days pass, I worry more and more, especially as the holidays draw to a close.

'Mummy, when are we going home?'

Mummy has that look which says she will speak and there's to be no comeback. My tummy starts squidging … tying itself up in knots.

'Cherub, this is Home now.'

Eh?

'This is where we will live as a family from now on.'

Eh?

Her voice is firm. No mutterings, no arguments. And definitely no questions …

'But what about Charlie? I mean … he's waiting for me … he won't know … and the goldfish … the fruit in the garden … my swing … we left them behind …'

'We have one another. That's what's important. We're a family. Daddy is studying to be a Minister. We are responsible to the Church …'

I've no idea what she means. The only words I hear are that we're not going home. No Charlie in my world any more.

The next morning we leave my sisters behind. It's a different journey, but the same place waiting at the end of it … *Hospital*! It confirms my worst fears.

We've left our lovely little bungalow far behind … and the garden … my secret den … school … people I have grown up with … and Charlie … Everything that was familiar is no longer there for me now.

My world falls apart, and I'm never quite the same person again. Something in me dies.

Mum's diaries explain:

1962
It was on 23rd April 1959 that Jack arrived home from work to declare without preamble or discussion, a 5 year plan for Ministry and the financial implications. Once he had outlined this plan he retired to bed, leaving me alone with my thoughts. Now it is happening for real. But not soon enough for Jack, it seems.

He has been staying in Wiltshire where we were to join him later. But unexpectedly he returns home, saying we are to come now. The bungalow they are building for us isn't complete, but a couple who belong to the church are moving out of their home and offering it to us until our own home is ready.

Selling our bungalow means we will have £2,000 to last us the year. Meanwhile Jack will need to pass every examination to maintain a roof over our heads. Financially it has become increasingly difficult to make ends meet. Money remains scarce. Jack will work part-time at Bulford Army Camp to help make ends meet.

The hospital have been informed and Janine will continue to visit the Specialist where treatment will continue.

School is a little wooden shack in the centre of a village a walk away from the house. The headmaster lives next door, and there is only one other teacher. I am introduced as 'the new Minister's daughter', and, with a sense of shock, I discover that, apart from everything else, I have changed my identity. I am expected suddenly to be knowledgeable about Jesus and the Bible. I creak up the aisle in my hospital shoes to read prayers in assembly. Readings. Scripture. *'Mill on the Floss'*, *'Silas Marner'*, *Miss Read*.

'Come on, girl. You of all people should understand the Lord's Prayer. Your father is a minister ...

It's a completely different way of life.

I'm a completely different person to the little girl who lived on a hill.

Suddenly it matters what people think. How we dress. How we act as *'Children of the Manse'*. Lights have to be switched off after using them to save electricity. All telephone calls recorded. Minimal heating. I supervise my sisters. Take them walks along the river running through the village to spend pocket money at the shop. All the time I yearn for the life I've left behind – when Daddy was just 'my Daddy' and not Daddy to everyone else.

One day, I arrive home from school to find those crates in the hallway. This time I know what they mean. The game is 'Moving'. In days we move a few short miles into a newly built bungalow close to Dad's church. Now the village school is almost next door. All our subjects are indicative of village life. The changing scenes of nature around us are reflected in our work - nature rambles, tree rubbings, collecting leaves and pressing them into books.

But then I'm hardly settled, it's only been a few months, the year has just turned to 1963 following a long harsh winter, and we're moving again ... this time to a busy housing estate the other side of the borough.

Ten years old. I hate moving. I feel like an alien moving from one planet to another. The only thing that remains the same is my title '*Minister's Daughter ... with the funny leg*'. It's so hard to fit in, to make new friends, forever wondering when we'll move again. And all the time there's this pressure on me to play a part, to be someone else, to fulfill other people's requirements of me.

But then the bullies are something else.

'Have you heard the latest by The Monkees?'

Why don't I simply say no? Why lie? It only means digging a deeper hole. But then I want to fit in, to be like them ... to be accepted ... to be one of the crowd.

'Oh yeah. It's the greatest, isn't it?'

The minute the words are out I realise what comes next.

'What's it called then?'

'Er ... Got my mind on other things right now, but tell you tomorrow.'

I can hear the giggles behind me, the door closing on my trap even as I make a mad dash for home hoping somehow to find answers. But then I'm always one step behind.

'*Last Train to Clarksville.*'

'Name another.'

'*We're The Monkees.*'

I was prepared for that one!

But then …

'Impressive! Okay, we'll give you that. So which track do you like best?'

A quizzical look. I'm staring off somewhere into space, but the answer was already in my head.

'*This Just Doesn't Seem To Be My Day.*'

My look now is one of triumph! I've done my homework. It took me half the night, listening to Tony Blackburn on Pirate Radio underneath the bedclothes on a trani I got from a jumble sale.

'Well done! So which track is that from which album?'

'Oh.'

I'm done, all out of knowledge. I can't remember. I don't know. I don't have any Monkee records anyway, and I never will have.

My record player is a hand-me-down from Dad, an old beat up green box with a lid that sticks every now and again. Our only family collection of records range from '*Home on the Range*', to '*Stranger on the Shore*' by Acker Bilk, Glen Miller Collection, Vera Lynn, and Nina & Frederick. My pocket money is spent on music I can play and sing on the piano, old time music to entertain in old folks' homes and hospitals.

They're not impressed.

There wasn't anything in which I could get involved, socialise, make friends.

'Come cycling ...'

I didn't like to tell them I'd got a large three wheeler from a jumble sale, given I couldn't keep my balance with my legs.

'Come to the Lacarno, ice skating ...'

'I can't ... *I can't ... I can't ...*'

'Why not?'

They knew full well why not. They were taunting and teasing, having fun at my expense.

'I've got a bad leg.'

Finally, they dragged it out of me.

*'Janine's got a bad leg ... a bad leg ... a bad leg.
Janine's got a bad leg ...'*

It becomes the new school chant, taken up whenever they see me.

Meanwhile, hospital visits continue … plaster casts … I break my leg trying to roller skate to get to the Lacarno … trying to get in with the crowd.

I wake in the mornings and carry a sick feeling through the day. Panic and dread fill the pit of my stomach. It's as if something bad is about to take place. I come home from school via the cake shop on the corner. There is always a special cake for each of the family, their favourite, when I arrive home. But then there is another bag which I carefully hide away in my wardrobe. It's comfort food for when I'm alone. There's a name for it … *'Bulimia'* … when you feel out of control in your life … cramming sweet food into your mouth and then making yourself sick. So here I am, rushing home from school to cram food into my mouth as a source of comfort, filling the hole, the aching, crying Need. Then later, feeling overwhelming guilt, I make myself sick. I'm confused about the way I am, confused about my body. I'm confused about me. I'm growing up when I want to be 'Peter Pan'. I yearn for childhood and carefree days walking in the cornfields, playing on the swing pushed by Charlie. I have fears about growing up and changes I see happening. I want to halt progress. What I see I don't understand. And there's no-one to explain. There is nothing to make sense of why I feel so bad.

Why do I feel bad? Why do I deserve to be punished when all I've ever done is to try to be a good girl?

It is 1967. The crates are back in the hall. We're moving ... to Northampton. New beginnings ... and my very first pair of real shoes. I am attending a Girls' School. Lunch means picnics in the park. I am in a class of nine. It means catching up on lessons, catching up on friends. The past is gone. Forget the past. I'm singing in a church choir, giving concerts at hospitals and clubs playing keyboard and guitar. My name appears in the papers. I'm getting noticed.

'Have you seen that Dave?'

'No. But I had a fantastic time with Greg last night.'

'*Mmmm* ... he's dishy. How about you, Jan? Who do you go out with?'

Boys ... boys ... boys. What do I know? Me! Who's never had a date and never been kissed. Always the odd one out. My life revolves around church meetings. Church outings. Church concerts. Church socials. Church choir practice ... and music ... and cake!

A letter arrives from the hospital informing us that one of the two Specialists treating me has died.

The bad one? Oh please God, make it the bad one! Please please bring some justice into my little world?

But no ... it's the good guy who's gone. I am now in sole charge of my abuser ... the Greek.

51

My stomach is doing somersaults. The old familiar dread creeps in and up through my body, closing tight around my heart. All around me and within I see and feel Green ... Green is taking control ... closer ... closer ... closer ... tighter ... tighter ... tighter ...

'*No! No ... no ...* **NO**! I'm not going back any more. I'm done with hospitals and Doctors and Specialists and Surgeons.'

And as an afterthought:

'You can do what you like!'

I refuse the final operation on my foot. I've had five operations to date. All have been equally unsuccessful. *Why should this one make any difference?* I know my leg and foot well enough now. I can manage the way it is. I still have to wear special orthopaedic shoes. I can't change that. But otherwise ...

I AM ON STRIKE!

I am adamant I will never return to the Hospital again.

A chapter ends in my life.

For the first time ever ... *I have taken control*!

Colour me Purple

Our greatest source of learning lies within our selves

The church is throwing a party to welcome the new minister and his family. I have this new woollen dress and it itches like crazy. Tables of food hug the walls. People jostle and laugh and chatter. It's a profusion of sound and energy. So many faces, too many names to remember. I just want it over, for us to go home.

A Youth Club follows after. *Oh please no, please don't make me go?* It will mean trying to fit in ... trying to please ... to be accepted ... to ...

'If you're going to San Francisco ... you've got to wear some flowers in your hair ...'

Music is playing, words I don't know. But I like them.

'Knock three times on the ceiling if you want me ...'

'Let's drink a drink a drink to Lily the Pink the Pink the Pink the Saviour of the human race ... '

... and the haunting harmony of *'A Whiter Shade of Pale'*.

'Fancy a dance, love?'

'Er … sorry, I don't dance.'

'What d'ya mean you don't dance. We not good enough for you … *or what*?'

'No offence. I just don't dance … can't.'

'Okay, Dave. Dave … let's play games … Dave?'

'Right … what game do you want?'

Dave was in charge. It was getting late. I was watching darkness fall around the windows, a cloak of safety into which I might disappear. Now if I could just slip out to the toilet … out in the passageway …

'*Spin the Bottle* … everyone knows *Spin the Bottle*!'

I watched a bottle pushed to the floor, everyone sitting cross legged in a circle around it. There were more boys than girls. Everyone was looking at me.

'*What?*'

'Start the game then. You're the newbie. We're waiting for you to start.'

'What do I do?'

'Spin the Bottle … you know? It's a game. Where have you been all your life?'

Smirks all round.

'She doesn't know, does she? Okay, we'll need to *educate* her. This should prove fun.'

After a few turns, I can see the way it's going … and it's coming my way. Already I'm counting the number of steps it will take me to get to the door … and away. But then …

'Okay, the bottle is pointing at you … let's see who you've now got to kiss … or is it you prefer to take the forfeit?'

'I don't know … I'll see what comes … decide then?'

A chorus of '*ooooohs*' starts up around the circle. I'll take my forfeit and then make my excuses and leave. After all, they can hardly keep me from leaving against my will.

'Bill … the bottle is pointing at you. Do you want to kiss the lady?'

Bill has a hairlip. I've never seen anything like it. I'm not sure how I'll cope if he comes near, let alone tries to kiss me.

'Er … what's the forfeit?'

'Doesn't the lady want to kiss then? Hear that Bill … you're being turned down.'

Bill isn't happy. In fact, he's in an ugly mood.

'Erm … I need to go now …. I'm leaving okay?'

Brave words!

'*Chicken!*'

I head for the door. They watch me go. I feel like I just failed an exam. Nothing new there. But how will it fair for the future? I only just met these guys. I need them on my side.

Darkness swallows me up.

The pub on the corner is throwing people out. Together with the shops opposite, they light up the streets. I know I have to just cross the road and head down the street opposite to find the house we now call home.

A shadow dogs my footsteps. I walk quicker. It walks quicker. I walk faster. It walks faster. A figure appears at my side. The voice whispers into my ear:

'Shall I carry your bag?'

I ignore the approach and continue on.

'Are you shy, or something? What's the matter with you?'

An arm winds around my shoulders. I wriggle away.

'Come on, now. Loosen up a little, lady.'

'Leave me alone, can't you?'

At first I'd thought it was someone following me out of the church hall. But this was a stranger. I'd never seen him before. Caught in the dark, he had form and shape and an eerie kind of familiarity. We approach the corner and I turn for the first time to face him.

'What's all this about? What do you want?'

'Naïve, aren't we?'

Then he kisses me in the full light of a street lamp, pushing me hard against the post. I freeze.

'Want to go to the Pictures?'

Now outside my gate, the light from the window gives me courage I couldn't find before.

'Would *you* like to come in and meet my parents? Have a coffee ... *or something*?'

'You what?'

The figure disappears rapidly down the darkened street. The shadows swallow him up. But ...

He's kissed me!

I'm pregnant!

A baby is already wriggling in my tummy, shifting, shaping, preparing its way into the world! I'm going to be a Mummy very soon!

Naïve, vulnerable, afraid, I am sixteen years old.

A child.

I have no idea how babies are made. Periods came as a shock. I thought I was dying. I kept it secret until an aunt came to visit. She bought me my first bra. But this ... *who could I talk to? Who would tell me the truth? How could I find out for sure if this baby was soon going to become real?*

Colour Me Red

The Hurt keeps us looking back
for as long as we keep hold

Bill arrives at my home one evening the following week. I don't even like him. He has a hair-lip, an untidy crop of thick wiry ginger hair, his skin is pocked, and he is dressed in scruffy attire with a pair of tatty jeans hanging halfway down his thighs.

I am happily watching a movie on TV. An old black and white weepy where the young RAF Officer lovingly wraps a greatcoat around the shoulders of his sweetheart, telling her in the loveliest way how much he loves her, before joining his Unit to fight in the war.

A series of sharp knocks on our front door brings me back to the present with a jolt.

Damn!

I miss the ending of the film, sitting in the cold back room, listening to '*Top of the Pops Chart Show*' on the radio. I never listen to '*Top of the Pops*'! It isn't a part of my world. I collect old music and newspapers from the 30s, 40s and 50s. But then you can't turn a visitor away, it seems, however much you don't like him or don't want to get involved. Mum says I must make friends. We're going to be here some time.

To help the situation along, Mum brings soft drinks and biscuits. I just wish he would go … and quick. He makes me feel uncomfortable.

'Come on, it's cold. Come and sit up here on the sofa by me.'

'I'm okay on the stool, really I am.'

'No, really. Come up on the sofa by me. Come on …'

I'm not being coy or a tease. It isn't some kind of female plot to make him want me more. I've never been this close to a boy … except Charlie. Oh, to be with my mate Charlie right now!

I've just had my sixteenth birthday. I feel as if he is an alien invading our home. Home is safe. Home is loving and safe and special. It's still very much like being part of a fairy-tale castle, with Mum and Dad the King and Queen, and nothing can spoil the magic that is ours. I live in an unreal world … the world of a child. I don't want to grow up. It's a dangerous world of which I don't want to be a part. In my world, I can be anything I want to be. And that's okay … as long as I stay within the confines of Home. It's a bit like Red Riding Hood sticking to the path through the wood. The dragons live outside. But they don't touch our world.

Bill − he isn't part of Us. He doesn't belong. Besides, *I … don't … like … him*. If it wasn't for Mum and politeness gone mad he wouldn't be sitting here with me now, and I wouldn't be missing my film.

'Look, it's getting late!'

'Oh, come on, it's early yet. We've got plenty of time to get to know one another better.'

The only trouble is, he isn't talking. He's getting impatient for me to join him on the sofa. Getting to know me seems to mean getting to know my body, and I don't know how to respond.

Mum pops her head around the door.

'Okay? Anything else you want?'

Yes, yes, YES! For this guy to go and for me to be left alone! I plead with my eyes.

'All right, all right ... I'll leave you two alone. Just shout if there's anything you need. I'll only be next door.'

She misinterprets my signals.

'Okay, I'm not taking no for an answer. I'm not leaving until you've come up by me onto the sofa ... See, that's *so* much better! Nice and cosy. Just we two. Now snuggle in ... that's a good girl. You were silly to sit shivering so long on the stool when we could have spent more time like this.'

At the risk of him staying longer, I shift position and do as he says. *Always be polite to the guest!* He moves to kiss me. It's not so bad ... not really. But as I feel his hands begin to wander up and under my skirt, pulling at my tights, abruptly I push him away.

'Okay, okay … I get the message. It's time to go. I'll get my coat.'

He snuggles the RAF coat around my shoulders. I remember the war hero doing the same for his sweetheart, the man on the bench in the film. I find myself playing the part.

Suddenly, I'm caught in the movie. He's kissing me under the stars on a moonlit night by the gate.

And I know I'm going to see him again.

*   *   *   *

He calls at the weekend to ask me out for a walk beside the canal. It's a fine day. He's leaving the following day to return to the RAF. Mum makes us a picnic. It's a strange feeling walking beside a boy for the first time … well, a man really. He tells me how he is ridiculed at the RAF camp where he is stationed, hounded by the authorities, always getting extra duties for having dirty boots or not shaving. He is an outcast. Different. We identify, talk about Home. He lives with his grandparents and elder sister. His parents are divorced. His father is married again, with children of his own. His mother left him for her parents to bring up, and they meet infrequently, sharing a love-hate relationship.

It's a strange set-up. He intrigues me. I want to ask how it feels, what he might say to his Mum given the chance. As he talks about her he sounds angry, hollow, empty, as if someone has sucked out all emotion. How can such a relationship work? What problems might it store for the future?

'When I applied for the RAF it was an opportunity to get a proper education. Something to do with mechanics. I'll start out an apprentice, but it's good money. I'll be able to travel home regular. It's a way of getting away from THEM!'

He spits out the words. 'THEM' presumably refers to his grandparents. I'd learned they were strict. Old-fashioned. He was a bit of a loner. Sporting a moustache, an attempt to cover his hair-lip, I gather he's had his share of bullying.

'The RAF says I can get my hairlip sorted if I want. They'll pay for the operation. Having it done with them means I'll get the best attention.'

I'm concentrating on what he's saying, my thoughts in a whirl. I don't immediately realise we've left the path leading alongside the canal. Suddenly, he's dragging me down beneath a tree.

"Hey! Hang on a minute! You're hurting ..."

Stupid! My immediate thought is that this is the place for the picnic. But the bag has momentarily disappeared. He's playing ... having a romp like we're kids. I think of Charlie at the little bungalow I left far behind when I was nine years old.

But this is something different.

Hands grope inside my dress. It's a short just-cover-the-bottom mini I just acquired from a recent jumble sale, white spots on dark blue … typical sixties attire. I feel the zipper at the front give. He's crushing me with his weight, clamping me down by my hair, holding it tight so I can't see, my head jammed between the ancient roots of the tree.

It's Autumn. Leaves on the old oak high above my head are just turning … yellow, the lightest of green, golden brown. A sudden gust of wind sends a flurry of leaves on my face. My hands are caught behind me. With a growing sense of horror, I watch him awkwardly unzip his front. His fingers and nails are dirty, blunt, savage. A hand forces my knickers off while the other maintains a grip on my hair, holding my head to the hard unforgiving ground. I manage to free one hand which flails helpless, a flag of surrender, desperately trying to get a grip, to be rid of this burden on me.

A memory stirs. I can't think … can't feel … can't speak. I am a child again. Mesmerised by the patterns of leaves above my head my mind blanks. All that I'm left with is the pain, the humiliation, the shame – and the restless image of the Autumn leaves stirring against a clear cloudless sky.

Crisping leaves fluttering like confetti around a young couple squirming on the ground. Behind them lies the still murky waters of the canal, crisp packets, empty beer cans and cigarette stubs float on a clogged surface matted with waste. Further back stands the blackened factory wall, a monument to times past.

'I found my love by the gas works croft, dreamed a dream by the old canal, kissed my boy by the factory wall ... dirty old town ... dirty old town ... I'm going to get a good sharp axe, shining steel tempered in the fire. I'll chop you down like an old dead tree ... Dirty old town, dirty old town.'

Just as the child traced a journey around the white tiles in the bathroom, unsure what was happening, whether I was going to hospital or school and who was taking control; now quietly I whispered the lyrics to a 60s song I played in concerts, driving away the evil feelings of the moment.

Somehow I arrive home dirty, blood trickling down my legs. I look like I've been dragged through a hedge backwards, and then some. Entering by the front door I'm afraid someone will see me. *How to explain the unexplainable?* And yet I'm half wishing they do see me. But then there is laughter from the front room over something on TV.

'Is that you, Cherub?'

'Yes, Mum.'

'We're in here when you're ready ...'

I go straight up to my room, strip off clothes suddenly unclean, run a scalding bath. Nothing can rub away the dread seated heavy in the pit of my stomach. *Where did these feelings come from? Where do they belong?* Somehow I've lost track ... time is lost ... my mind blanks ... the day is gone.

Later, I sat in an easy armchair, my family around me, feeling so alien, so lost, so removed. There's an old black and white movie, capturing the essence of a love caught and held between a woman and a man. But it catches and snares on my sub-conscious because somehow I know … it isn't like that … not really. Films and books … they lie. And it's so easy to believe the lie when it offers such magic and emotion. You want there to be so much more, and so you imagination, and aided by the pictures and the story, it makes it happen right there, while you're watching or reading, drawing you in, making you a part of the lie. Stories stop at the point: *'and they lived happy ever after'*, for a reason. It's so you never find out the truth.

'Don't touch down there!'

'Good girls don't play with themselves.'

'Bad girl, pull your dress down straight, sit up, hands folded in your lap …'

Early pictures flash through my mind … Charlie and I at the bottom of the garden … *'I'll show you mine if you show me yours …'* We were playing. That was all. But you would have thought it was the crime of the century the way I was punished by being locked away alone and abandoned in my garden. It was wrong. It was bad. I was wrong. I was bad. Years and years later, Mum said she was afraid for me. I was *'sullied'*. Charlie had *'sullied'* me. She wanted desperately to separate me and Charlie … *'for my own good'*. She was also scared my two sisters would go off with the 'Barrack Boys', the Army just across the way. This seemed to be a root cause for us moving.

Colour Me Orange

Freedom is a state of mind

Summer holidays come to an abrupt end.

Breakfast one morning there are two sets of papers waiting at my place at table. The house is unusually quiet. My sisters sit, heads bowed, spooning cereal into their mouths as if their lives depended on it.

'Well, if you'll excuse me ... must get on with work ...'

Dad slides his legs from under the table and hurriedly exits, on his way to the study. The door quietly closes behind him.

'Come on, girls. Hurry up. There are jobs to be done remember?'

Mum tries to get my sisters out the way.

Curious, I lift one of the papers, taking a peek, my stomach lurching in that oh so familiar way, as if telling me be careful, something big is going down, and you're not going to like what comes.

Waverly Hall
Boarding School for Ministers' Daughters

'Mum?'

'Now don't jump to conclusions. You have a choice. Read through the leaflet. It's very good. We can go and have a good look round to make certain.'

'Boarding School? Me? Why?'

I'm being punished. It's my immediate thought. They want me out the way. I'm too different, I'm never going to fit in. There's nothing else left, no way to be a part of the family. They're sending me away.

'It has an excellent write-up ... and music particularly is praised.'

'But it doesn't have to be music I do for the future. I want to go to Tech. You know I've been asking for their brochure. It isn't far away. This place you're looking to send me ... it's the other end of the country!'

'Now come on, we're not sending you away. We're trying to do what is best for you. To provide you with a good education.'

'I want to go to Tech!'

'That isn't an option!'

'I left school earlier this year. It was the end. I've had enough. I took O' levels and passed English at least. I want to write ... to become an author.'

'Now Cherub, you need to be realistic, to live in the real world. But it's your choice. There is another option.'

She's nodding encouragingly at the table. I push aside Waverly Hall papers, completely mystified why they would want to send me there at all. If I can't go to Tech, I'll get a job. They can't hold me back forever.

Nelson Bennett Grammar School

'What's this?'

'It's the Curriculum. It's very good. Again, it has an excellent reputation. It means you can continue music and go on to become a musician or a teacher of music at least.'

They had it all planned out. It just wasn't the way I wanted to go. So why, one week later, did I find myself sitting opposite a headmaster, my mother resolute beside me?

'You want to be a what?'

'A writer, Sir ... an author? Someone who writes books?'

'I know full well what an author is, young lady, and you've obviously got your head in the clouds. There is a real world out there. You can't go around with such fanciful ideas. ...'

A gaggle of girls giggle at a group of boys across the way. Skirts hitch up as high as regulations will allow, and then some. Perfume bottles do the rounds. Eyes gum up and hair fluffs out. Hips sway, long legs flash tantalising in dark coloured tights. It could be a scene from *West Side Story*. But as they move around, slowly forming a circle, closing in, the spotlight is centred on me.

Lizzie King, Queen of the Bullies, there is nothing to touch her. She has absolute power. Even the staff bow to her command. I enter the gates of a morning and no matter how early or how late, there she is … waiting. In the centre of the playground with her cronies, everyone else who enters looks to her for a lead, and remains still and silent. Then the hissing begins … a hissing which is taken up by everyone, boys and girls, while the teacher on duty goes inside. No-one intervenes. No-one heeds my desperate pleas. I am at their mercy. Doorways and exits are blocked. I stand, befuddled, confused, not knowing what to do to make this awful world go away.

The Head has placed me in the lowest class two years younger than myself because I came from a Comprehensive Education. It means re-taking 'O' levels before going on into the 6th Form to continue with music.

'*SSSSSSssssssss* …. ', like serpents they hiss about to strike.

I recoil in fear.

'*SSSSSSssssssss* ….' the hissing comes again.

Faces appear at windows. I am caught between. There is no way out.

'Ja ... nine, Ja ... nine, Ja ... nine ...'

When the bell rings for the start of school things don't get any easier. Feet trip me up in the corridor. My coat is snatched and hidden. School books crash to the floor. When I go to sit down, the person behind pulls the chair from under me. The teachers don't seem to know how to take control. It's a game of cat and mouse. And all the while I'm being baited into a trap.

A crash of brick breaking glass. A jagged hole in the classroom window. Someone scribbles *'Janine did it'* across the blackboard. Enter teacher. The chant begins:

'Janine did it ... Janine did it ... Janine did it ...'

'Who broke the window?'

'Janine did, Sir.'

Thirty nine out of forty say she did.

'Look, I'm sorry to have to do this. I know it's not your fault. But what else can I do? You can see the way it is ...'

Detention ... for something I never did!

R.E and Games are worse.

'She wants to have sex ... she wants to be kissed ... she wants a boy ...'

The chants go on. The teachers, unable ... unwilling? ... to contain the rabble. Quietly they tell me it would

71

be easier if I didn't come to lessons. Where do I go then? Oh, don't worry, they'll mark me in, but if I go to the toilets it would make their jobs so much simpler. I have a note excusing me from P.E and Swimming and Games. Changing in front of the girls and showers is more than I can stand. Besides, what will they say when they can stare openly at my foot, my leg, my body?

But then, a Rescuer from an unexpected source ...

The consequences are dire!

Colour Me Brown

There is no shame in being Child
- as long as we don't allow someone else
to take Control!

She is special. He knows it from the first moment of
their meeting ... special because he knows her need,
and therefore the emptiness in her life he can fill.
'Special' becomes part of the secret they share. As she
enters his class, he begins grooming her for what is to
come.

A victim in the making ... ripe for the picking. And
she's a good girl, used to obedience and rules.

Just sixteen years old, vulnerable, unsure how to
relate to peers, locked inside an alien world, afraid to
confront, to assert, to simply say '*No!*' head down,
shoulders slumped, I walk in shadow ... isolated ...
alone ... insecure ... afraid ... still very much the child
seeking acceptance, reassurance, love ... shrouded in
'*happy-ever-afters*', locked in false promises of
childhood and artificial dreams ...

Abandoned, betrayed.

He guides me to my place at a desk at the front of
his music class, an empty desk in front of his own. I
feel his eyes watching as I fumble for the right books

and, looking up, he presses his lips together and nods, a brief curt show of approval.

He sets the class work, and sits beside me as if it's his right, using the empty chair at my side, placing his guiding hand over mine, gliding it slowly down to my knee. It remains there … skin on bare skin … I don't know what to do, what to say to make it go away. It's wrong. He shouldn't do this. But I'm sitting at the front of a class. How can I do anything without it being noticed and causing a scene?

As if I've passed the first test, he offers a reassuring pat and moves away from the chair. My relief is short lived. Moments later he stands behind me, hands hovering across my shoulders, protective, possessive even, parenting the child I have become.

'Any time you want to use this room, that's fine. You have my permission. Lock the door behind you to ensure privacy. Break times and lunch you can come here and practice. No-one will interfere. And I hear you're not taking part in PE, swimming or Games … would you like me to put a word in for you, to allow you to use the room during those times too?'

He wasn't so much asking as clarifying the way it would be. His room becomes a haven to avoid the bullies. Other teachers collude in excusing me from class. They're only too happy to release me into his care. Just by being there, it seems, I throw classes into chaos. Soon I am spending PE, swimming, Games and RE secluded in his spacious store-cupboard at the back of the classroom, able to finish work assignments unhindered, away from the taunts of my peers.

In turn, I learn what pleases him, what will earn a word of praise. I come to depend on his approval as an addict does a fix. At first, it's the little things ... tidying, giving in a neat piece of work. Wearing my sister's shorter pleated skirt guarantees me the right to play the piano, my preferred instrument, in the orchestra rather than the flute. Wearing my hair loose instead of tied back in a pony tail, walking and sitting where I am more accessible, letting hands wander, means his door is always open. He has even made it possible for me to use the teachers' entrance to school to avoid episodes in the playground. While under his care and protection school bullies are thwarted in their attempts to attack and to ridicule me, which they continue to do through classes I attend.

Sixteen days after my first day at the school he talks with my parents:

'I'd like to offer your daughter Janine private music lessons at my home. I understand she has been taking the Associated Board, and we can't let her special talent go to waste. I don't have time at school. But in the privacy of my home we can do so much more ...'

No choice. No discussion. It is a *faite accompli* ...

'Oh Cherub ... how wonderful! What an offer! Of course, there's no question. I've already said yes. You'll start next week, a couple of evenings. He says it will be best if you take the bus. Have some independence, instead of Dad calling with you in the car ... Why so glum? Aren't you pleased? It's a truly golden opportunity and more than we could have hoped for ...'

It's a trap … a trap which snaps open … snaps shut … becomes everyday routine.

I catch the bus after school, barely having time to snatch something to eat beforehand. Up the hill, crossing the road at the corner, walking up to the gate, the couple of steps up to the green enamelled front door with the polished knocker. *Why does it have to be green? What's that about? Why the gnawing dread in the pit of my stomach kicking in?* I don't remember, but it settles like a hard lump of iron, putting me on edge. This is the kind of area that feels safe, good to live in. Houses are detached, inviting. Suburbia at its best. And yet behind the door of number 6 is a secret no-one knows or could even imagine. Not even the family living next door. The school teacher and his wife and young daughter make a respectable family. An integral part of the community, he is a composer, creator and conductor of the Youth Orchestra and Cathedral Choir. They attend church regularly besides putting on musical events.

'Hello Janine. Come in. You know the way ...'

I gaze at the little girl clutching her mother's skirts … his daughter, his wife … and I wonder … while being led through the hall and on into the room beyond. I sit and wait in the ante-room, watching the door, just as I did as a child, sitting in the hospital waiting room, mesmerised by the green door behind which sat the specialist. A memory lost. But the feelings were there, fragmented, nagging, churning up dread within.

Usually there is silence. Sometimes a piano plays. Finally, a young girl with plaits slides out, a shadow joining the night. We catch one another's eye as she turns at the front door to gaze with a tear stained face behind her. I'm counting the number of steps to join her … to leave this house … when …

'*Janine …*'

A hand beckons. His figure stands in the doorway. Hands hover around my shoulders, holding, pressing me to him, slowly drawing me out of my coat, eyes undressing me further. I feel hot breath on my neck. Hands fondle, stroking my hair. There is an urgency, a neediness emanating from him. His tweed jacket tickles my nose as he pushes my face into it just after I see the familiar beads of sweat break out just above his upper lip. I've seen them before, in the classroom. I don't know what it means. But always, always fondling, handling, touching follows after.

The cushioned seat in front of the piano is long enough to sit three or four bottoms never mind one. *Or is that the idea*? I play my practised pieces for perhaps ten, maybe fifteen minutes. Scales follow. He sits beside me, strokes my arm, pats my knee, guides my fingers across the keys. Then abruptly, he stands, moving behind me. He massages my shoulders, sensing the tenseness, moulding, making me his own.

A knock at the door. His wife enters, the little girl still with hands clutching her mother's skirts. No word is spoken. A tray is pushed onto the low coffee table in front of the sofa … and she is gone.

I want to cry after her, beg her stay, say something, anything to delay the moments that follow. *But what can I say? How can I stop the inevitable? Where are the words ... for her ... for my parents when I reach home?*

There is never an exchange of words other than about music. That's why it would be so easy to make believe it hadn't happened at all. Just like the specialist ... only I can't remember ... at least, not then. He frowns, knitting deep dark eyebrows together, nodding meaningfully at the couch. I delay, fingering the piano keys, gazing blind at the manuscript on the stand. He waits ... knowing I will come.

My fingers trace flower shapes on the sofa, just as a child I traced the tile outlines in the bathroom in the house on the hill not knowing if we're going to hospital or school. He is sitting watching ... unnerving. And as he reaches for my hand, nervously, I go for the teapot and begin to pour. It's surreal. A Mad Hatter's Tea Party. When tea fills the small china cups, too hot to drink, again, he takes my hand, holding it, pushing it across his lap to unzip his trousers.

I've never seen a penis. The rape by the canal has joined a collection of mislaid pieces of my life. I can't remember. And yet ... feeling stirs. Crazy images flit like shadows in and out my mind. They make no sense.

Beneath my hand is a rounded growing ball of ... I don't know. Even at sixteen years old I'm still a child. I don't understand. I haven't had the 'birds and the bees' discussion with either of my parents. It has never been a part of my growing experience.

He pushes my head roughly into his tweed jacket, smothering, choking, sickening, while he guides my hand to pull his pants and hold the sticky writhing snake-like 'thing' within his trousers. *Please God, let me go. Please God, let me die ...*

But God isn't ready to take me just yet.

Only once did I ever jerk my head free of his hand and pull away with the words:

"Can't we just do the scales?"

"Can't I just play this piece ... and go home?"

The plaintive pleas of a frightened child released into the silence. He let me go. With a deep frown creasing his forehead, he opened the door to my cage and set me free to go home.

Next day at school his door was locked to me. I became fair game to bullies who did their worst. I sat in the toilet, taking off my tights, preparing to throw them over the rail close to the ceiling, standing on a stool, tying one leg around my throat, and hanging myself. I was so deeply traumatised and unhappy, so unhinged by everything that had happened to me I couldn't quite grasp or understand.

For three years I endured in silence the music teacher's humiliating games both at home and at school. I failed my 'O' level deliberately to exclude myself from his class the following year. Somehow, I was still put forward for 'A' level, forced to endure further and further acts of depravity and sexual abuse.

Bullying grew worse as I entered lower and upper sixth. My parents couldn't afford the correct school uniform. And the lining of my obligatory grey jacket was a very obvious deep orange. Mum had made the suit using old stock of material.

At the age of nineteen years old, I left the jacket hanging on the chair of the music teacher on my final day. A statement ... a finger stuck up in the air at my abuser. He would know it was mine. There wasn't another like it. And with a last look at the walk-in cupboard at the back of the classroom in which I'd spent so many miserable hours, and my desk at the front where I'd first been targeted and groomed ... I walked away, believing that part of my life was over ... finished ... done.

I failed both my 'O' and 'A' level music, as well as Grade 6 of the Royal Associated Board of Pianoforte Examinations.

It seemed my only chance at taking back control ... at saying a very definite '*No!*' to both my parents and to the abusing teacher.

Afterthought

It wasn't until thirty years on and then some, I discovered I had a choice.

Why didn't anybody tell me?

It's a shock to realise my life could so totally have altered ... if only I'd taken control.

And yet at the same time, I know why I could not ... why things had to take their course.

In an age when children respected and revered their parents, in an age when saying '*No*' wasn't an option, at least in the majority of households, at fourteen years old I went on strike as far as the specialist at the hospital was concerned and refused point blank to return. That hospital never saw me again, and throughout my life I never returned to treatment for my 'club' foot.

My grandmother with whom I was very close, lived alone in a very large house. *Why did I never think to say I would go to live with her?* She went on to develop dementia and was found wandering outside in her nightdress, taken into a Nursing Home, and died there. Perhaps I could have slowed the progress. We only saw her once or twice a year, but she and I corresponded constantly. She was lonely, widowed for 39 years. She was always telling my parents I was being treated wrong at the hospital. It was she who found my cream cake and chocolate store as a bulimic teenager. With her nursing experience … *she knew*! We shared secrets. I could have made a different life with her.

More recently, through *Friends Reunited,* I came across a girl who attended the same school. But after just two days she refused to go back. She said it was intolerable. And then she added: 'You were sixteen years old when you went there, in a class two years your junior. Why did you accept ill treatment? Why stay when things were so bad? You would have been entitled by law to simply walk away.'

I didn't know I could. I was never given that option.

From an early age I was controlled.

It isn't a blame game. I loved my parents dearly. It was an era where you held your parents on a pedestal and they could do no wrong. I could think of them in no other way. Did they betray my trust? Did they let me down? They did what they believed was right at the time out of love. They protected me, they believed, by keeping me ignorant of the ways of the world.

But by that very fact, they failed to show me how to protect myself.

Discipline and control. It's a fine line … especially when you are a good girl. And very confusing when you're trying to make sense of your life!

Colour Me Gently

Life isn't about living – it's about Experience!
And it's what we take away from each Happening
that says how the rest of our life will be

Life outside school was equally upside down and inside out, fragile, confusing, filled with past images and pain. Nothing made any sense.

Somehow yearning for love ... *made it love?*

I spent long evenings by the phone, willing it to ring. When it did I'd crawl right up the line:

'I'm sorry, love. I won't be home for your birthday like I promised. I've been put on 'Jankers' again for dirty boots and long hair on parade ...'

'I'm sorry, love. My forty eight hour pass is cancelled. I don't know why. Could be something to do with not ironing my kit properly ...'

'I'm sorry, love ...'

'I'm sorry, love ...'

When he did get Leave, he'd meet me outside school and I'd feel so good at the way everyone stared and commented at his handsome RAF uniform ...

But then ….

'*Dishonourable Discharge*' from the RAF.

'Too good for them,' he boasts and sets off to find a flat. All I can think about is finding him a good home and being together.

But why?

I'm not stupid!

I am all kinds of a fool!!

We find a bedsit in the centre of town. I take a book-keeping job, on leaving school, and every evening after work hurry back to prepare a meal. He returns from the factory, changes, eats, and disappears into the night. In his absence, I wash his clothes, rubbing them by hand in the sink, clean his room, tidy his wardrobe. Later, I sit reading romances of how love should be.

… waiting for Life to take hold.

* * * *

1972
The landlord stands solidly at the foot of the stairs.

'You can tell your boyfriend he's out. He's not paid the rent in a month, and you can clean the place before you go. Do yourself a favour. Find yourself a real man.'

I race up ahead of him. The sink is full of vomit. Beer bottles lie about the floor. Clothes collect dust in a corner. I gather them up and put them away. In the wardrobe is a pair of size 12 tights and bra. Not mine. Later, I confront him with them.

'Oh, I bought them ages ago as a present ... for you. I wasn't sure if they were the right size so I opened them. They weren't, so I pushed them to the back of the wardrobe. Should have got rid of them. No harm in that, is there?'

Bill is quick to defend his actions. *Has he someone else? What does he do when I go home? Where does he disappear after dinner?* I do not voice my suspicions. I dare not question for fear of losing him. And we leave it at that.

But again ... why?

Why not simply walk away?

I was worth so much more.

If I was to meet myself as I was then, an almost twenty year old, I'd give her a few home truths, for sure!

'I don't like him, Cherub. Why don't you find someone better?'

'Look at the way he's treating you! There are plenty more fish in the sea.'

Mum and Dad made their feelings clear.

'Bring her home by ten.'

'Spend the night in with us playing a board game.'

I write words in my dairy:

> *'They seem to be deliberately forcing us apart. I resent their interference. I can make up my own mind about things ... and be right! I'll prove it. They have made all my decisions for me. Now it's my turn."*

*   *   *   *

1973

We meet outside the Children's Home. It's as if I placed myself in care after leaving school. I answered an ad for a Residential Care Assistant. I have my own room in a purpose built building. With three different units grouping like ages together, I work in the Nursery, abused, battered and abandoned children up to the age of five years old. And I think nothing of walking down to the park with nine children. I seem to have found my niche. Quickly I am moving up to Assistant Supervisor. Another unit works with juniors, the final with teenagers up to the age of sixteen.

I'm part of a different family now.

'Come on, let's go for a drink.'

'I'd rather stay in tonight and do something together?'

'Oh, don't be such a bore!'

'Look, why do we always do things you want to do and never seem to take into account my feelings?'

'Little Miss High and Mighty is it now? Give me money then and I'll go and leave you alone.'

'No.'

I'm getting brave. Finding a voice. Teenagers at the Home don't like him, don't like the way he treats me. They are coaching me, urging me not to give him money which he'd simply drink away.

I'm worth more … or so they tell me.

His hand leaves a burning streak down my cheek. It isn't the first time.

'I haven't got enough to last the week as it is.'

'Sod that!'

His hands feel hard and merciless as they hit me around the head. In trying to duck out his way, I trip over a stone and fall to the ground.

'Take that, you tight-fisted bitch!'

His foot kicks where it hurts.

'Bill? Bill … *stop it*! You're hurting me. People are looking.'

A couple across the road pass as if with their eyes shut. It could have been an everyday occurrence. Don't get involved! He leaves me where I have fallen. His long legs carry him on down the street, around the corner, and away.

'Bill? Bill … wait for me … please?'

For one fleeting moment I think of going home. But Bill seems the only chance I have of breaking free, of being free, of forging my own path. I catch him up at the crossroads. Together we walk into the pub.

He buys me a long cold lager to make up. It tastes bitter. I don't drink lager. I hardly drink at all … Two packets of crisps and four bags of peanuts later he leaves to buy a box of my favourite chocolates from the shop.

'Here you are then. Don't say I never buy you anything.'

But then, hang on, whose money was this?!?

* * * *

The Children's Home put on a party for my twentieth birthday. We put the children to bed then congregate in the main hall for cake and drinks. Bill arrives … he's not just late … but drunk. He bangs toy drums, belts bedroom doors, creates havoc, annoyed that the party is now coming to a sudden close. No-one wants trouble. But the children are awake, confused, distressed, crying at the noise going on around them. And in the middle of it all, Bill flakes out.

'Why don't you leave him, Jan? He's a real louse.'

'Better the devil you know than the devil you don't.'

What suddenly makes me so wise? What do I know?

The truth is, I'm scared – scared of being alone, of being without anyone at all, scared of simply being Me. I don't have the confidence, the feeling of self-worth to live life a single person. Besides, isn't this all I'm good for? Isn't this all I'm worth?

Colour Me Black

I dreamed a dream
In which the earth went black
And the world began again.
I dreamed a dream
And all was changed
And nothing remained the same.

'Janine, will you take Bill … to be your lawful wedded husband? Will you love him, comfort him, honour and keep him in sickness and in health, as long as you both shall live?'

On 19th January 1974 my father's voice reverberated around the packed church. People stood still and silent, holding their breath … the final commitment, signing away my life. The end of my experience as a battered girlfriend – trailing along behind him like an after-thought, submitting to beatings in the street and at his bedsit home – and the start as a battered wife.

The person you do it with first is the one you marry. Isn't that right? Bill won't care I'm tainted and sullied. Maybe I need to be punished for letting my parents down … allowing so much pain and badness into my still young life. And then again, fairy stories, fantasies, childhood dreams, the promise of *'happy ever after'*. Marriage changes everything, doesn't it? No more beatings, no more lies, no more hurt. Love conquers all.

No-one ever talked to me about what happens after. It's all good, even if it wasn't before.

I adopt the mindset. This is my Destiny. I listen to the words my father is speaking ... and believe.

Standing right there at the altar, my mind swirling with thoughts, I look down at the wedding gown I'd found in a charity shop, £12.50, with bell sleeves. It isn't what my parents had wanted for me, but then, what did they know? I watch his leg jiggle beside me in his secondhand suit. He's nervous. It means he's taking his vows serious. I wish he'd speak up so everyone could hear and know that he is accepting his responsibilities as a man.

At the back of the church are the children from the Home. Every now and then little Mark's voice breaks into the proceedings adding a note of relief. In the centre of the church are friends and relatives from all points of the compass. Soon they will be gone except for the odd birthday and Christmas card. Ahead is the choir. 'Uncle' Harry stands straight and tall and proud. Many are the evenings spent with him and 'Aunty' Kath. Aware of my inner conflict, my turbulent emotions, they have their doubts about this wedding. Harry gives a secret smile and links hands with Kath. A shining example of true love ... a second love each of them discovered at the age of 78 years.

Behind me, my two sisters stand like sentries on point duty. The youngest holds her posy like an Olympic torch, blushing the deepest of reds if anyone looks her way. They have giggled in corners throughout my turbulent teenage years, keyhole conspirators, trying to catch a glimpse of what their own future might bring.

Mum stands as one alone, her anguish private. A sad smile betrays her role as proud mother. The tears sliding down her face show the heartache she feels inside for her firstborn. But suddenly, I know. These aren't the tears one would expect from a mother on her daughter's wedding day. There is nothing happy about these tears. These are tears of deep sadness ... and a knowledge, a fear, reaching far beyond present day.

I have a sudden urge to giggle. My shoulders shake. I fiddle with my veil to hide my embarrassment. Tears sting my eyes. I am crying. *What the hell am I doing? This isn't a game, for God's sake! This is my life right here for all to see.* I want to laugh crazily, to turn and run down the aisle, out the door and away. *What is the matter with me? Stupid, stupid Child ... grow up, why can't you! Make a stand before it's too late. Do something, anything, to take control before it's all too late.* My emotions are running riot. In the corner of my eye, Bill stands erect, a stranger at my side.

'I do.'

The words could have been firmer, louder, said with more conviction.

'I do.'

I hold my breath, expecting a thunderbolt to shatter the heavens, a fanfare of trumpets ... anything. But a heavy deafening silence echoes around the church. *The Wedding March* is playing. With a gold band locked around the third finger of my left hand we walk out of the church doors into a new dawn. I catch Mum's eye, just for a moment. She smiles sadly ... and I look quickly away.

* * * *

February 1974

Now I'm a married woman I'm no longer living at the Children's Home Our flat is at the top of a three storey building in the centre of town. Bill is working nights for extra money so I am alone most of the time. Long dark silent nights ... nights that haunt and terrorise and fill me with such fear.

I lie beneath the covers, clutching a water bottle for comfort on a cold winter evening. I am woken suddenly by footfalls on the stairs. I'm waiting for the stair before the landing because it squeaks. But it doesn't come. No sound. My whole body strains in the silence. *Is someone there? Shall I go look? But what then?*

Other times the footfalls sound, and the second to top stair squeaks. *No! Who ...?* Bill is working. I've asked him before if he's come back from work, and he says no. *So who? How?* And then it comes ... the heavy weight on my chest ... the body lying on top of mine ... the stink of drink ... the sweat ... the hard rough hands ... and the long silent scream while he rapes me again and again and again ...

Do I pass out with fear? Do I sleep? Is it really happening to me? Have I finally lost my mind? Again and again Bill denies ever coming back during his shift. So it's me. Told enough times it's easy to believe it's true. At the time, it's so real … so awfully painfully real. And yet from childhood, I should know that nothing is what it seems.

I remain tense, nervous, on edge. I see a figure in every shadow. Foolishly, I open and shut doors, peering petrified into cupboards. I can't sleep as long as there's a chance someone else is in the flat.

I can't sleep anyway.

Seven until ten o'clock stints at the new Children's Home down the road are exhausting. I got a transfer into an ordinary house in an ordinary street where children are treated like a family. It's a close knit community. But of an evening I arrive home when Bill has already left for work to find the flat in chaos … a note will say the rent man has called wanting payment, placed beside a conglomeration of dirty dishes, cigarette butts, broken crockery, beer bottles scattered about the floor.

*　*　*　*

March 1974
Row to end all rows.

Sparked off as my engagement ring, a single solitaire diamond, bends and then breaks in half. Bill is in a frisky, playful mood. He has been demonstrating judo techniques picked up in the RAF … *on me*!

'Well, what did you expect for fifty pence? Real diamonds? Come on, get real!'

He laughs.

'But … but I thought …'

Stupid stupid girl … what did you expect!

'You thought what?'

He is taunting, challenging, hoping I'll take the bait. Standing over me his hands grip my shoulders in a vice and then he's shaking … shaking … shaking … my teeth rattling and rolling … my jaw hanging loose. I feel just like a rag doll about to be torn apart.

Suddenly, he releases his hold. I topple backwards limp over a chair. He moves to the other side of the room and sits smoking, watching me through slit eyes.

Dangerous!

Be very very careful …

I think back to the only time when we called time on our engagement. He was living in the bedsit, about to make his usual exit after dinner. I asked him to stay … plead with him even … asking to talk for a change … share an evening together.

'I'm fed up with waiting around for you when all you do is fit me in when you have time. Give me some attention instead of giving it all to drink. Make me feel like I'm really your woman … someone special … someone you truly love.'

I remember the words.

'*You're* fed up! I'm sick to death of your whining, woman. Give me that ring and clear off. I don't care if I never see you again.'

It was my ticket home. Blinded with tears, I took everything I paid for – food, pots, pans, crockery, cutlery, even clothing. Now he would have to come to me when he wanted something … and on my terms. I was finally seeing sense. Being strong. He had no money. I'd only to bide my time. He'd be sorry. It would all come right in the end. New beginnings, that's what this was all about.

Why did I always have such high hopes … and then be disappointed over again? Why couldn't I simply accept the truth?

At home, tea and sympathy.

'You're well rid of him. He never did treat you right, Cherub. Let me make you more tea.'

I wished then my parents would say nothing. They meant well, but it made my indecision worse. They didn't know the way it really was. And still I was afraid of being alone. Of starting again. My sisters had boyfriends. Why was I such a failure, a freak? Why couldn't I make a relationship work?

'Hello. It's me. Can we meet?'

Silence. I'd knelt, huddled in the downstairs cupboard with the phone, speaking in whispers so no-one would hear. It was early morning. I didn't want anyone to see what a perfect fool I was.

'Hello … hello?'

'What the hell do you want?'

Not the response I'd expected, but at least he'd answered. Another five minutes elapsed. I coaxed and wheedled. Finally he relented, grudgingly.

'Okay then. I'll meet you by the river tomorrow at noon. But this time we get together on my terms.'

His words … not mine, the way they should have been. What happened to my determination, my resolve? I was weak, pathetic, a stupid, idiotic woman who was living in cloud cuckoo land. Wanting the prince, the knight in shining armour … while all I really had was the frog.

I was right there, waiting, like the sucker I was. My original ring had been lost over the past few days. I wondered if he'd sold it to buy food. But then again that would be my fault. I took everything he had. He'd bought me another to replace it … 50p from the market … and we resumed from where we left off.

Except …

I was outraged.

Fatal!

Never show weakness, especially to him, especially now when he's in such a dangerous mood.

'You bought my engagement ring … *from the market*?'

'That's what I said. You deaf as well as stupid? I needed the money for other things.'

I lost my cool then. Used words I'd never even thought of using before. He'd brought me down to his level and I hardly recognised the harsh, vulgar voice as my own.

Then the blows began.

'You bitch! I'll show you who's boss …'

He retaliated in the only way he knew, and I became a punch ball. His hands punched my eyes, nose, mouth, until they looked a bloodied mess. A knee came up to buffet my stomach. I sank to the floor winded, gasping, breathless. A slave kneeling before her Master? I'm drained. Desperate. This isn't the way it's supposed to be, the way I'd been promised in childhood.

My fingers found a hold. I pulled, punched, kicked, determined not to be beaten. Usually I kept a low profile, submissive always. But this time … well, this time it was different. I was different, so incensed that my feelings grabbed hold and wouldn't let go. All the anger that had been building up in me for so long came gushing out, a torrent, a tsami of emotion … my legs were black and blue with bruises, my arms, my body, my head and face … everywhere I hurt. But above all else, it was my pride that had taken a pummelling.

The row ended abruptly. He slammed out the flat and didn't return.

I cleaned up and crawled belatedly into bed in the wee small hours of the morning, pulling the covers over my head, blanking out the world … the cruel, hateful, horrible world. *Where was this beautiful world I'd been promised as a child? Where was the 'happy ever after'? Two months married. Disaster … but then, where can I go?*

A scream rang out. My mind snapped back into focus. The bedroom. I covered beneath the sheets. The scream came again, followed by breaking glass. Voices raised in anger. Then …

Silence.

Bangs and thumps. Pat and Ray downstairs were having a fight of their own. It seemed to be the area for it. I'd never seen or heard couples act this way with one another before. It was frightening. And I was an integral part. I turned over to bury my face in the pillow, plugging my ears … and slept.

Something cold and clammy clawed at my clothes.

I tried to push it away, believing it still to be part of the nightmare. But it wouldn't go away. What was worse, it came closer. Hot breath panted on my face, bristly stubble rubbed my cheek, irritating the skin. Fingers sticky with sweat moved down my body.

'Bill … Bill is that you?'

I tried to catch hold, but my arms remained pinioned to the mattress.

'Stop it, Bill. You're scaring me.'

I'd become a writhing, wriggling worm, working my way to the floor.

'Wazzat?'

Drunk. He was drunk. A hand reached down, feeling, searching, stabbing. I lashed out, a tormented tigress – clawing, clinging, scratching.

'Un-freeze, Ice Maiden. I'm going to get what's due. It's time I had some fun.'

He found ... held ... hurt.

I felt used, like a whore, a prostitute, someone he'd picked up off the streets. This was brutal, rough. This was rape. A scream rang out in the night. This time, it was me. It came from a place deep within. I didn't expect it not to hurt. It always had ... always would. I just thought it should be somehow different? Books I read made it out to be so much more than this. But then books always did that. Books lied.

Life was better after that ... at least for a while ... luring me into a false sense of security. Until the next time. I began to believe life was on the up and up, that Bill had somehow miraculously reformed. He was sorry for that night of terror. He'd been drunk. It was the alcohol talking. On bended knee, no less, he asked forgiveness. And yes, I forgave. Why not? He was my husband of two months. I blamed it on the way we were living. It would be different if the Council gave us a house. But then again, I blamed myself ... always ...

May 1974

'Our love has been put to the test several times over,
these past months, and it is hard to believe there
can be any harder test waiting for us in the future.
Yet this has to be, for we cannot pick the rose
without the thorn. Much as we would love life
always to be bright and beautiful, we need the bad
and the ugly to help us appreciate what we do have
all the more.'

9 June 1972

Bill is arrested.

We retire to bed early for once, celebrating the end of the three day week. I'm still trying to overcome my fear of having Bill in the same room, never mind about being next to me or touched. I am just starting to untense a little when there is a pounding on the front door.

'Who's that?'

'Dunno … I'll go see.'

He returns somewhat sheepish.

'I have to go to the station.'

'The station? Now? Why? Where are you going?'

'I'm going to the police station. Don't worry, I won't be long.'

I haven't quite come to grips with the situation.

101

'Wait a minute, I'm coming with you.'

The next couple of hours I'm listening to an account of how he and two friends have been joy-riding in a stolen car. Bill has been driving. Bill? He can't drive! But he's the one caught and they need the names of his accomplices.

It's a change to see Bill wriggle. I've not seen it before. Under pressure, he cows in the face of authority, pleading with them to keep his name out of it if he 'grasses'.

'We'll see what we can do … Sir. Now then, you were saying …'

16 June 1974
Burgled … my guitar the only item taken. But I'm shattered. It's my one escape. My one means of keeping sane. I feel so alone without it, like a part of me is gone.

Bill is nervy, edgy, staying in more than he did before. I fail to see the connection. I'm just grateful for the company, especially now when I feel so low. Finally then … finally he's coming around … understanding … wanting to make amends for the past … loving me the only way he can.

23 June 1974
Bill arrives home from work badly beaten. A visit from the police follows. My guitar has been found in a second hand shop, hawked by two accomplices to teach Bill a lesson for 'grassing' on them. He refuses to press

charges. But hang on, it's *my* guitar! I'm the one suffering, not him. Don't I get to press charges given it's my property? It seems not.

Bill is taken into custody for non-payment of a forty-pound fine.

I'm still living in Cloud Cuckoo Land. I bail him out of trouble with a forty pound cheque just received from work, meant to last the month.

'I'll pay you back, Jan … honest I will! You're a real gem.'

The money goes out on permanent loan.

1 July 1974
'Dear Mum and Dad,

Thanks for putting up with us over the weekend. It was wonderful to get away for a while. I'd loved it to have been longer … a lot longer. I wish you could understand how I feel. I know I have hurt you by marrying Bill. But I have never gone against you before in my life. And in this I still feel right. It hasn't been easy. But then, I never thought it would be. With him I have grown up. I am a woman now. I have experienced life. We have our arguments, but doesn't everyone? Please try to understand. Accept me for what I am. It would mean so much.'

4 July 1974
My 21st birthday.

Do I feel different? This is the very first birthday I've celebrated outside my family home with Mum and Dad. We hold a party which rapidly develops into a right royal boozy affair, increasingly out of control. Bill and a couple of friends take centre stage. My sisters and the couple from downstairs leave early. I sit quietly alone, watching the scene in front of me play out until the end when they collapse into chairs and are silent, the record stuck, the needle grinding away. Mince pies, pasties and cake turn to crumbs. Beer bottles pile high on the floor. I sit some more. Then bed.

Colour Me in Tears

Listen to the child within,
act on what she knows,
often she is wiser than the woman

12 August 1974
a.m

Just saved my first hundred in the bank, after weeks of going without tights, meals, treats … It is a proud proud moment as I enter my last three pounds on the white giro slip and hand it over the counter with the notes.

p.m

Bill finds my cheque book. He demands I give him money to buy a car he's seen, adding a few well aimed kicks for good measure. A threat of things to come. His boot reaches up to thud into my bottom. I turn and yell, an animal in pain, and he cracks my knee. It gives under me, and I'm falling to the floor.

'There'll be more where that came from if you don't.'

13 August 1974

I'm so damned proud of my bank balance, the way it's mounted up slowly over the weeks. I can't let it go now. I simply can't. I keep out of his way all day, leaving for work early, arriving home late. But then ... he's waiting ... just as I should have known he would be.

'Don't say I didn't warn you.'

I'm finding out the hard way that it's best not to show it hurts. If I scream or shout in pain he'll only do it more. I feel like an animal being tortured every which way just to see how I'll react ... and then trying something more.

'*Bill ... stop it*!' I scream, as he bats my head off the wall. Each time it makes contact I believe it's the last before I pass out. A fisted ball punches air out my stomach. Vomit comes up in my throat.

'*Bi ... ll!*' I choke on his name.

He doesn't speak a word. His fists and feet say it all for him. I grit my teeth. Swallow painfully. Dig nails into the palms of my hands until they raise blood. Anything to take my mind off the agony of it all. And only when he's gone ... run out the flat and away ... can I cry quietly to myself, hugging myself in a corner of the room like a small frightened child.

14 August 1974

I wish I hadn't tried to be brave. Now I have the additional shame of walking down the street with a black eye. I keep to the shadows. Turn my face to the wall. Look away if someone tries to speak to me. But still people stop and stare.

'You've been in the wars, haven't you? What did the other fella look like?'

The cashier peers close. I stammer something about walking into a door, and walk quickly away.

Bill has a smug smile on his face as I meekly hand over the money.

'But what's the point of buying a car when you can't even drive?'

Stupid girl ... stupid me! I never know when to keep my mouth shut. A stinging slap catches the side of my cheek.

'I can take lessons, can't I? Now shut up, woman. Who are you to tell me what to do?'

He leaves without another word ... or action. Once more I am left alone counting the cost.

15 August 1974
5.30 am.
My pillow is soaked in tears. I look for a car outside that might be ours, correction *His* ... but there is none. Puzzled, I put on the kettle. The fridge is stacked full of beer cans. I find Bill lying on the sofa in the front room. The remains of a Chinese take-away spatter carpet and chairs. His sleeping fingers still hold a cigarette butt. It has burned holes in the cushions, dropping ash on the floor. I kneel to take it away ...

Glazed eyes stare at me as if I am a stranger. I search for that spark of love that must be there ... somewhere. He must still be suffering the after effects of drink. But then slowly, slowly he focuses ... and smiles. My heart skips a beat. How easy it is to please me. How stupidly I cherish the dream.

I lean forward to offer a kiss. Roughly he pushes me away, pointing to the far corner of the room.

'See ... see what I bought? I had a real ball last night.'

Almost two dozen rock records lay by the stereo. Hundreds of cigarettes are stacked neat in two piles beside them. On top is a box of chocolates. My reward?

'Have one ... go on, have one if you like.'

He looks proud. I choke back tears. What's going on? I feel like just one more possession he's grown tired of.

'What happened to the car?'

'Oh that, I changed my mind didn't I?'

He's like a child who's been given too much pocket money.

'Anything left, any change?'

He laughs.

'Never give up, do you? Just enough to buy my mates a beer or two at dinner, that's all.'

I hesitate before asking the obvious.

'What about work?'

But there's an answer for that too.

'It's raining … or hadn't you noticed?'

He doesn't go to work in the rain.

'Lend me bus fare, will you?'

I turn abruptly, grab my coat, slam the door hard behind me. Some of us have to work whether we feel up to it … or not.

* * * *

6.45 am

A wall of noise hits me as I step through the door.

'Hi, Sal,' I greet the night nurse.

'Morning, Jan. Like a cuppa?'

I appreciate the offer and the tea, smiling ruefully as the bedroom antics begin over again.

'Been like this since six,' says Sal, striding towards the nursery unit of the Children's Home.

'Hey!'

Her raucous voice bounces off the walls, makes children suddenly sit up and listen.

'That's enough!'

'It's okay. I'll go in to them.'

'Right then, I'm off. Bye.'

Sal never looked back. The outside door swings shut behind her. I feel trapped and so alone.

'Anni Jan.'

Michael. Baby Michael. One and a half years old. There are some compensations …

'Anni Jan?'

A deep breath … I open the door and plunge into another day.

The room is a mess.

'Darren! What do you think you're doing?'

Darren stands and stares. Baby blue eyes choose to ignore the neat pile of screws in one corner, his collapsed cot in the other. He's the nuts and bolts expert … just three years old.

'Linda … come away from the window. Phil, put away those books. Mary, pull Graham back out from under the bed, there's a good girl …'

Stop the world I want to get off … !!!!!

* * * *

8 am

We reach the breakfast stage.

'Dick, please try to concentrate. Put some egg on your fork … that's it! Good boy! Now, hold your head over your plate and … NOOOOOO!'

Yellow yolk spatters the walls. Dick giggles. Twelve years old with a mental age of three. I suppose he tried. Paul, up in his high chair, decides to follow suit, and soon egg is flying in all directions. I pick a blob of it from my hair and clear the plates. After all, this is just an ordinary day.

* * * *

Playtime

We adjourn to the main hall where a slide, a rocking horse, and various forms of plastic transport and box of toys wait to be abused. Mary and Jean have left for school with the others and I worry about them as if they were mine. But they're tough, they've had to be to survive. Their mother is a prostitute.

I step back into the nursery, mechanically clearing, washing, drying dishes … sorting, mending, making beds with envelope corners.

'Don't you say anyfink 'bout my Dad, you fucker! He's the best, he is …'

Words of abuse hurtle to and fro outside. I hurry back to the hall.

'Mark! Stop it … stop it now. You'll hurt him.'

111

I grab an arm and leg from the tangle of bodies writhing on the floor, dragging free the kicking, screaming, shouting boy.

'He called me a liar. He said my Dad was …'

'Mark … Mark …'

We fight our way back through the bedroom door and fall together on the first bed we come to. I sit and rock the frustrated form to and fro on my lap.

'He didn't mean it. He doesn't know,' I soothe, stroking the sandy-coloured hair. He cries then, hiding his face in my lap. His father is in prison. His mother can't cope. He's being penalised by his friends. They don't understand … how can they? His hard headed exterior is just a front to hide the deep deep hurt he feels inside.

* * * *

11 am
Coffee break.

I clear a path to a seat to sit down for the first time in two hours. Orange is passed around the children. They munch happily on biscuits. Dick sits cross legged on the floor, playing with his willy through a hole in his trousers. His shriek of laughter suddenly makes the girls giggle. His laugh is infectious. His face baby smooth, naïve, innocent … no sense of betrayal there.

My head aches. I finger the lump rising at the back tenderly, remember the night before. A bruise is turning black on my arm. I pull the sleeve of my jersey down to hide the evidence.

'Coming to the party tonight, Jan?'

Neil works in the teenage unit of the Home, easily likeable, easy to talk to.

Yes … yes … yes … I'd just love to come!

'No. I'd better get home. Bill will …'

'Bill …? *Ugh!*'

He looks like he has a bad taste in his mouth and passes on out through the swing doors into the sunshine beyond.

* * * *

1 pm

Dinner: beefburgers and chips. It's the children's favourite and they clamour for more. I try not to notice the way Mary's knife and fork form a cross on the table. She is praying. Michael watches her nervously. Brother and sister, both brought up devout Roman Catholic. The others tease them about their faith. But their mother has died recently, and aware of their loss, I treat them like fragile dolls.

'Mary … have some pudding,' I chide gently.

She raises her head. Our eyes meet. I can't help feeling strangely disquieted by her direct approach.

113

'Dick! No more mess … please!'

I turn my attentions elsewhere.

A walk in the park means Michael and Paul seated in the twin pushchair. Darren holds one side, Dick the other. Mark romps ahead to let everyone know we're coming.

'Push me, Anni Jan.'

'Lift me on the roundabout.'

'Tell Michael to stop kicking!'

It was chaos … bedlam. They were going mad, letting off steam.

'Give the boy back his ball, Mark. It isn't yours.'

'Come on. Come and get it, weakling … or I'll thump you where it hurts.'

Mark's bullying voice sends the boy crying to his mother.

'*Cry baby … cry baby bunting …*'

The boy's mother is looking furiously at me, focusing her anger.

'Look here, if you have to have this many kids, at least keep them under control.'

She storms out the park.

'Sorry, Anni Jan. I …'

'I know, Mark. I know. Come on, everyone. It's time to go.'

Red faced, I hustle my brood down the road, back to the Children's Home.

'One, two, three … where's Mark? … four, five …' I'm counting heads. Suddenly I'm one short.

But then …

We're taking a roundabout route, we've stopped at the shop for sweets. We pass the bus stop and I see a woman leap ahead of us. A bus pulls up. I expect her to get on board. Instead, she leans forward unexpectedly to drag Darren from the pushchair … and runs with him in her arms.

'It's all right … it's all right …' I calm the panicking children.

Should I leave them and give chase? She's jumped on the bus as it leaves the stop. I reach up, but her arm just pushes me away, jarring my already bruised body. I think I'm going to throw up and be sick. But then, I can't … not in front of the children. The bus moves out of sight.

'Come on, all of you.'

I walk with them slowly back to the Home and near to tears report the incident. It seems it's been on the cards that Darren's mother would try to snatch him out of care. I just wish I'd been told of the dangers.

*   *   *   *

4.30pm
Jam sandwiches and cake for tea. Even Dick manages on his own. The children are hungry after our day out. I take a breather and two paracetamols, trying to kill the throb in my arm and head. If only it were as easy to kill the pain of my life!

'Jan … can you get another cot ready? We've a late arrival.'

The children sit happily in the TV room as I unfold sheets and set up the small bed.

'Jan?'

I take the bundle offered. Pam, the Superintendent comes to help.

'Found in a phone box is all we know,' she explains as we wash and dry the thin crumpled form.

'Poor little mite!'

*   *   *   *

5.30pm
I begin to run baths. It's been a long day. My back aches as I bend over Dick, the last of eleven. He's in a playful mood. Water splashes over the side and he kicks, catching my bruised arm. I'm almost screaming in pain.

'Dick … Dick behave!'

He giggles in that innocent way he has, and I wonder at the idea that he will always be this way, never grow up, never have to make decisions or have family and home of his own. I leave him sitting on the potty to check on the others in the bedroom. Darren is busy taking his cot to bits again. I jerk it back to the wall and tuck him in for the umpteenth time. Mary needs to say prayers.

'God bless Daddy. Keep him safe. Don't let him get lonely. God bless Michael and me. And please God, make Mummy happy with you in Heaven.'

A lump catches in my throat. I kiss her tenderly goodnight. Again, those all-knowing eyes unnerve me. But then I remember Dick in the bathroom.

'Oh no … Oh Dick … what have you done?'

I whip the boy quickly off his perch on the edge of the bath. He's been busy in my absence, giggling at his handiwork. Brown lumps of shit smear the walls, dripping down onto already soaked mat and floor.

One hour on, I finish the floor and begin washing down walls. Tears of frustration edge down my cheeks. I brush them away. I have no time. Sal, the night nurse, arrives to find me shovelling the last of the shit into a bucket.

'Oh Lord! I can tell what kind of a day you've had!'

But I can't speak. I just need to get away … and quick … disappearing onto the last bus … and home.

* * * *

Over the next few weeks I become a shadow of my former self. I eat, sleep and work, keeping my emotions on a tight rein. Bill believes he's beaten me into submission. He is boss. I play my role of dutiful wife and things slowly wind down. I suppose I need something to pull me back to the reality of what my life is really like.

* * * *

23 September 1974

I return home late after a particularly gruelling day at the Home. I've been on my feet since seven o'clock this morning. My head hurts. My feet throb. Longing to sit down, I trudge the stairs. The flat is in darkness. There's no sign of life. Fumbling with the keys, I open the front door.

Black smoke billows into my face.

The acrid smell stings my eyes. Within seconds, tears are streaming down my cheeks. I feel for the light switch, fling the door open wide, wade through the smog to open windows beyond. In the kitchen, a blackened chip pan tells the tale. Hot fat has oozed off the draining board and congealed in the sink. On the cooker, a burner glows angry. No time to think. I race downstairs to the couple on the ground floor. Yes, they know what's happened. Bill has been down earlier, pale and shocked, livid his moustache was set smouldering. They'd given him hot sweet tea … and he'd left for work.

Outside, the air smelled sweet. I walk to the nearby phone box, dial the factory number. Several extensions later I am connected to his boss.

'Is this an emergency?'

I explain the situation and let him judge for himself.

'I'll have him sent home directly … in a company car. He should be about half an hour.'

As promised, a company car arrives with Bill inside. And as soon as he sets foot in the flat he starts.

'What the hell did you do that for? I could have done without the lecture from the boss after you tittle-tattled on me. I'll be the laughing stock tomorrow.'

The smoke clears a little, revealing walls of every room bar the bedroom covered in black dust. The floors are filthy, the furniture full of soot. He beats me up there and then in the hall … and I let it happen. How could I not? I knew it would come.

I topple backwards as he pushes me towards the wall. My head cracks hard on the skirting board. I bring up my hands instinctively to protect my face. But like a fencing partner, he aims instead at the undefended parts. *Wham*! A fist connects with the stomach. *Crunch*! A knee lands in the small of my back. Anywhere where it wouldn't show … that was the name of the game. My arms pinioned to my sides, he brings his body down on mine.

'You slut!'

He slaps my cheeks hard and they begin to burn. He releases my hands and I move them up to my face. But I've neglected to guard my bottom half. My pants are pulled off me and I'm fighting him every step of the way …

'Bill … not here … not now!'

'I'll show you, you cow. You'll do as I say.'

I wished I'd said nothing at all and simply taken the pain he dished out. I'd only made things worse. Forcefully, he shoves himself in position … *in* … *out* … *in* … *out* …the rhythmic heaving, the pressure on my body, it jars my nerves, making me feel sick … sick of everything to do with my life.

My bruised back is creased with pain. My arms are numb. I've promised to love, honour, comfort and keep him, in sickness and in health. It's my duty as a wife.

Besides, what else can I do? Where else can I go?

* * * *

24 September 1974
By 5 am I've washed the walls, brought some semblance of order to the place. Even so, the acrid smell remains. Bill sits smoking, watching my activity, dozing in fits and starts. At six, he demands breakfast. At seven, he goes to bed. At eight, I leave for work.

* * * *

December 1974

Approach to Christmas. A time for caring, for sharing, for love. At the Home I spend my days dressing presents in pretty paper and ribbon. At night, I return home to a lonely empty flat. Bill is always out … out with the boys? His friends? Drinking? I don't know. At this moment in time, I don't even care. Just as long as he leaves me alone.

The blare of a stereo from below blots out thought. Busy hands bake puddings, pies, cake. Keeping busy … busy … busy … prevents me crying. Carollers sing at the door: *"Be of good cheer … ring out the old, ring in the new …"* I'd had so many wonderful dreams of spending our first Christmas together. So where was the laughter … the love? Why all this pain?

I blow my last fiver on a tree and decorate it with kitchen foil, cutting out paper fairies. It brings back a little of the magic I remember from childhood. And on the spur of the moment I decide on a party … Christmas Eve it will be to see the big day in. I begin the task of cramming my larder with festive fare, taking pride in the things I bring from the oven. Bill will provide drink. No worries on that score!

*   *   *   *

Christmas Eve 1974

The night of our party. The flat is full to overflowing. Mostly Bill's mates with girlfriends, but I don't mind.

'More trifle? Another piece of cake anyone?'

'Swell party, Jan. Great food.'

121

The drink flows. By nine it's running out.

'I'll go get more. Coming, Dave?'

The two roll drunkenly towards the door and down the stairs. Suddenly, my smile is awkward. I'm so tired of the clamour, the confusion, the noise … fed up with being the proverbial wallflower, enjoying the occasion through others. Now I just want everyone to go home and leave me to mine.

'Come dance, Jan.'

Johnny. I've known him since the day he was best man at our wedding. A frequent visitor to our flat, I like him. He's a decent guy. I smile and turn away. But then he's sitting beside me, starting to talk, nothing special, just whatever seems to come into his head. And I find myself listening despite my hurting inside.

'Hey, Chris, put something soft and sexy on the stereo,' he calls, pulling me up and placing his arm gently around my waist. He can't know what it does to me inside. Nobody touches me that way.

'I … I can't really dance. I mean, it's all this jigging up and down that gets me. I never know what to do, where to put my feet, what to do with my arms …'

I hate to admit my inadequacy. I feel my face turning red as feebly I try to make a joke of it, moving back towards the safety of a chair.

'Come on, I'll show you.'

His voice is soft, soothing, gentle, and for moments we waltz awkwardly around the room.

'That's it, you're doing just fine,' he encourages, making me want to do it well just to please him, to say more nice things about me.

Someone refills my glass. It feels good. His arm is still holding me and suddenly, I don't want him to let go.

'Hi ... we're back! Did anyone mizz me while I waz gone?'

Bill. His slurred voice jerks us apart. The party splits up soon after. The last bus has gone long since, so Johnny stays over. Still on an all-time high, I twirl in to thank him for the evening.

'Come along now, time all good children were asleep and tucked up in their beds. Mummy's come to give you a goodnight kiss.'

I bend and kiss him lightly on the cheek. He jerks me down, his lips touch mine, igniting a spark deep within my soul. My emotions are on fire and confused, I pull sharply away.

'What ... what did you do that for?'

'Don't you know how I feel about you? I'd have had you myself if only I'd got there sooner ...'

Panicked, I'm fleeing the room, hot and hurt and crying ... fleeing the point at which it might have been, back to the present and Bill ... sound asleep and snoring heavily … sneaking beneath the covers, dreaming of a different life.

*   *   *   *

Christmas Day 1974
Johnny gives me a present of a woolly hat before leaving.

'And I'll be calling often to see you're wearing it … promise.'

I smile and shut the door. A part of me is held by a moment in time … living an alternate self … where the wonder and magic of marriage is real, creating memories of a better future, and the man and woman walk off into the sunset and live their happy ever after dream.

Colour Me with Truth

It's hard to leave a marriage with no real love because there is always the hope it will change and be different.

New Year Day 1975

This year, I want to stand up for myself. I won't let him put me down. I want to make something of myself, my talents, my music. I want to make my marriage work. I want to somehow fulfil myself as a woman. I want to find sex is exciting and everything it has ever promised to be in books and films. I want to have a child.

19 January 1975

Our first wedding anniversary. Lying in bed, I am tense, nervous, upset, crying. The voice raves on, shattering the silence:

'Why can't you be like other women? Look at yourself. You're a fucking mess … ugly, frigid, frightened … a complete and utter wreck. What a combination! What am I going to do with you?'

He stretches his long, lithe, naked body as if he's God's gift to women. I admire the ease with which he moves, the confidence, the strength. He is afraid of no-one.

'A man needs a woman to look after him, to service his needs ... to cook, to clean, to make love ... it's a fact of life. Didn't Mummy ever tell you about the birds and the bees? But what have you ever done for me? Eh? When have you ever satisfied me?'

He's dangerous, goading, taunting, pushing, hoping I'll take the bait. But no, I know him too well. I'm not about to make myself a target. He's just itching to lash out, to inflict pain.

As he starts towards me, I freeze. A rabbit caught in the headlights. I don't know any more what to do, what to say, how to be, or even what to feel. It's going to hurt no matter what I do. There came a point when I felt swamped by the suffocating protection and love of Mum and Dad. And yet, right now, I would give anything ... anything ... to be right back in that little house on the hill, a child. Mummy would make it better ...

'Okay, there's only one thing to do, one way to take it ...'

After, I cry myself to sleep in the spare bedroom. Hidden under the bedclothes I feel sick, choked, ashamed of the person I have become. I don't like myself any more. I don't want to live another day in this body. It doesn't matter how hard I scrub I will never make myself clean.

February 1975
My body is bruised and scratched. Red weals snake up my arms and legs, like tracks left in the snow. My face

is blotched. I've been self harming. Every mark on me I made myself. It's an unexpected turn of events. Now I slam out of the room during arguments … well, not exactly arguments because that would mean two voices instead of one. I listen behind closed doors while Bill quietly and viciously swears, effing and blinding about what he would like to do to me given the chance.

'Rotten bleedin' cow! I'd like to break her fucking neck. Bitch! All I want is some effing money …'

Somehow I've turned it around. I listen, before walking silently away into some private space to scratch and claw bare flesh, tearing it apart as if trying to reach that bad part of me and rid myself and be clean. If only I could dig deep enough in I could cut the bad out and become good again. Then I'm hitting my head against the wall over and over and over …

'Stupid stupid girl … stupid stupid woman … who the hell do you think you are anyway, taking on this monster, trying to make evil good when there's just no hope for either of you? It isn't going to work. And yet, I'm married to him. Somehow I have to make it work.'

He hates the idea he hasn't made the marks himself. Strange that he finds it so appalling, begging me not to harm myself this way. I hadn't planned it. Somehow it just happened.

'Please, please Jan … please don't do this to yourself. Your scarred body, it looks so ugly.'

Why doesn't he see it as ugly when the marks are his?

'A man can beat his wife. But it's just sick if she does it to herself. A woman has to accept who is boss. And if she can't, she must learn the hard way. It's not about punishing herself. That's the man's job.'

'But Bill ...'

'Oh shut up! Get on with my dinner and stop your blathering.'

I've started turning mirrors to the wall. He's told me so often I'm ugly I believe him. Told something often enough, you come to believe it's true. It's a form of brainwashing. And in the mindset of a battered wife, I'm ripe for accepting anything and everything. It's the way I am. Besides, I'm ashamed that whatever I do, however I am, I can't make this marriage work.

I look at Mum and Dad. Their marriage works fine. Dad doesn't beat her or cause her harm. They talk like adults to one another, each an equal, each respectful of the other. Never have I seen them fight. Rarely have I witnessed them argue. They fit together, like two parts of the whole.

I yearn to be cuddled, kissed, made a fuss of, respected, valued, bought a box of chocolates or flowers every once in a while, without it being some kind of reward for being a good girl and doing as she's told. What must that feel like? How might that be? It's just never happened to me.

Bill arrives home with a guitar. He's always envied me mine. Now he has one of his own. He twangs and twiddles the knobs without really understanding what he's doing. A string snaps and breaks. A curse follows. He takes money from my purse to buy another. The following week, he's bringing friends round to the flat. Johnny is amongst them.

'Hi Jan. Still wearing the hat and thinking of me? We're going into the Big Time, the rock music business.'

Every evening after becomes an all night sitting. They buy more and more equipment on HP ... speakers, amps and mikes ... the list is endless. Noise blasts through the flat and on down the stairs to neighbours below. White noise ... noise that has no notes, no melody, no music. It's deafening, distorted, demanding a listener's full attention.

At the end of the month, Hot Ayr has their first gig at the Carousel Club. Lucky I'm working! I can't believe people will actually sit and listen to this. I return home late of an evening to find the four band members drowning their sorrows, collapsed in a heap on the floor.

They're drunk, but happy drunk ... amazingly they are celebrating a resounding success. Two bookings for next month, and they're actually being paid. Fifteen pounds per gig. It's a start, they say. Now they need a new wardrobe of clothes. Work has been suspended for the time being ... for Bill at least ... he needs to practice. He's going to be a rock star. He wants to be pampered and told he's great. Flicking his roughened blackened fingers of his bass guitar is going to make him a multi millionaire!

And the stupid thing is, I'm jealous … *imagine!* I've been playing the piano since childhood, following through the Royal Associated Board examinations. I can read music and sing. My name has been in the papers following the exploits of concert parties I've brought together to perform at hospitals, old people's homes, churches, etc. I've even been in a folk band playing old sixties music. Now here he is, going out to buy a guitar just like that, a beginner … and being paid!

3 March 1975

On my way to do an all-day stint at the Children's Home. I'm late. Bill needed money … no change there. I had none to give and he didn't believe me, grabbing my purse, believing on finding it empty it's some trick to mislead him. He takes the few coppers then, desperate for a fag, makes me join him in a fruitless search of the flat. Post Office and bank books both prove penniless and he's forced to rummage in the waste bin for butts. *Ugh*! This doesn't please him at all. But then finally, finally I'm allowed to leave with a hefty push to see me on my way.

Suddenly, I'm on the pavement, face down, sprawled on the hard cracked stone. What happened? I don't remember tripping or falling. But then, this has happened before. Last week I fell and gashed my leg, laddering my tights. It's like I black out, suddenly and without warning. I had no choice but to phone work from a call box and tell them I wasn't coming in, then dazed, making my way slowly painfully home. I can't afford for that to happen again.

'Are you alright, my dear?'

A lady takes my arm, pulling me back onto the pavement. Somehow I've strayed into the road, in the path of oncoming traffic. I'm shaking from head to toe. I can't concentrate or focus on what it is I'm supposed to be doing, where I'm meant to be.

'I wasn't thinking. I'm alright, thank you. Really I am.'

I'm trying more to convince myself than anyone else. Somehow I drag myself to the Home where the Supervisor is kind and supportive. I can't keep from crying. My nerves are shot to pieces. My hands won't keep still as I sob out some of my troubles, jumping erratically from one thought to another. She listens, lending me 50p to get to the Doctor for a check-up. My mind keeps fastening on the fact I have a ten till eight shift to do to get paid. But she won't let up, seeing me onto the next passing bus.

'And don't come in tomorrow. Take the day off.'

I can't afford to. I knew I would be there, no matter what.

The Doctor is remote. He fiddles with his pad, plays with prescriptions, taps a pen on the desk. It's distracting.

'You know, young lady, you can't expect to get married and live happy ever after. That only happens in fairy stories. Everyone has problems, marital ups and downs, little tiffs. It's life. You come to expect it.'
He expounds his theories on marriage and I feel a fraud. I shouldn't have come.

131

'However', he continues, 'you do seem to have got yourself in rather a state, don't you? If you're not careful you'll be having a nervous breakdown. It has come to the point when you have to choose – on the one hand you have a husband and home, on the other work. It's up to you, of course, but I would concentrate on your home life and starting a family. I'll give you sleeping tablets and anti-depressants. That should help …'

His words give me plenty to think about. A child … a child will solve everything … wouldn't it? It would give Bill the incentive to be kind, loving, responsible … as a husband and a father. But then again, and now I'm looking at recent bruises on my arm; it could work the other way. What if he harms the child? What if I'm not around and he takes it out on our little boy or little girl? I know from working at the Children's Home how these things escalate, and what the end product might be.

I hand in my resignation at work. It's a gamble … I know it the moment the letter of resignation has changed hands. And oh how hard it is saying goodbye to the children. They've been my life for so long, part of my family. An ache starts way down in the pit of my stomach … these children so much a part of me, what might it be like to have one of my own?

And in resigning from work, it takes my independence away, offers me no monies of my own. For the future, I'll be completely dependent on Bill.

* * * *

20 March 1975

'It's just great having the little woman at home,' Bill boasts to his friends. 'It means I get to have a meal waiting on the table when I get home every single day … and all that home cooking … *mmmm* ….'

Perhaps I made the right choice.

And then, Lady Luck is finally shining on us, offering good fortune. We're offered, completely out the blue, a maisonette. We'd hoped for a house … maybe if I'd been pregnant? But the Council's official word on that is: '*You must have two children to be eligible for a house. However, after you've lived here a year, you can advertise for an exchange. Let us know either way what you decide and we'll arrange it for when the time comes.*'

All geared towards making babies, it seems. And there was me thinking it followed 'happy ever afters' …. But then again, maybe this finally is the making of us. A maisonette in a new housing estate the other side of town. We can get away from this area altogether and those who know us. Make new friends. A new beginning … oh please God a new beginning … without the pain of the past!

*　*　*　*

April 1975

'*Days are passing slowly. Each one feels like a year. I feel so old, so alone, so much more than my 22 years. Life has no meaning any more… no reason, no purpose. I just want to curl up and die.*

133

I'm staying in bed until noon, not bothering to dress. What's the point? Nobody cares if I live or die. I'm done with trying to keep myself tidy ... or the house for that matter.

Last week I made the effort. Spring cleaned and had a dinner fit for a king waiting for the worker when he got home. But Bill didn't feel like mince, potatoes, peas ... our staple diet when we were growing up. He threw the plate and its contents across the room, splattering the walls, messing the carpet. The chip shop provided for his needs. After, he fell asleep in the chair.

I feel so ashamed. He asks me at every opportunity why I can't be like other girls.

'... big boobs, that's what I like,' he tells me. 'Big boobs, cheeky bums, shapely waist and legs.'

And

'Have you ever thought of dying your hair blonde?'

I've taken to comfort eating, just as I did during my bulimic phase: bars of chocolate, mug of sweet cocoa to go to bed on, a pile of cakes, and sweets and .... Making myself drink jugs of water and then throwing up in the loo.

My depression has become a living death. And then, just when I feel I've reached rock bottom, there are a few feet further to fall. It's eating away at my soul, leaving me an empty dried out shell. I can't walk, I shuffle. My body is like lead. Everything is such an effort. My doctor continues to keep me dosed with anti-depressants and sleeping pills. They stop me thinking, stop me feeling, stop me hurting inside.

A woman across the way tries to commit suicide. She slashes her wrists. It's that kind of area. I feel her pain. Three children and a husband in prison. I watch the arrival of the ambulance that comes to take her away. Parallel lives. And suddenly, the thought takes root … *what if* … maybe that's the way. I have more than enough pills to be certain.

* * * *

2 May 1975
I count the tablets, spreading them over the table, a bottle of cider at my side. This isn't a cry for help. This is real. The pain is that bad. I can't live with it any more. And I can't see any other path to follow. No-one listens. Nobody cares. Why would they? It's just me.

Tonight I shall commit suicide.

Tomorrow I won't be here.

I'm in a drugged confused state. Pills begin to take an effect, powerful enough to fog my mind. I'm lonely. I haven't seen a soul in a week. I haven't been out. I haven't opened the door to anyone. I don't want anyone to see me, not the way I look now. Bill passes me as if I'm a shadow on the wall. We live as strangers.

Fleetingly, for moments the other day, I thought about leaving. It would mean going to my parents, saying I'm wrong, showing what is happening to me … and their expressions are more than I can bear together

135

with their rejection, hearing the word 'No'. I've almost kidded myself into believing this way of life is The Norm. Until now, I've waited each day, hoping Bill would walk through the door a changed man.

Persistent knocking brings me abruptly out of my reverie. My fingers are clutching a handful of pills as I answer the door. Why am I even bothering to answer? Who would I want to see now? But … I don't want to die alone.

Johnny. Suddenly I'm collapsed in a heap on the floor, crying as if my heart will break. The look of kindness, a gentle arm around my shoulder, the understanding word, it unlocks all the anguish I feel inside. He makes me hot sweet tea. Watches while I drink it. I feel all kinds of a fool. *What the hell do I look like? What must he think?* I cover my face with my hands.

'*Don't look at me, I'm ugly,*' I cry.

I don't really want him to go. To be alone.

'Why aren't I a real woman? Why can't I be wanted, needed, loved as a woman should be? What's wrong with me?'

I reach for the pills. But the time for that has passed. Things have changed. I have changed. We mount the stairs, stand together in the bedroom.

'Come here,' a soft voice is coaxing. 'I'll show you you're a real woman. Make you feel alive again.'

I'm walking towards the bed when the bubble bursts, and it's Bill, not Johnny, lying there.

'No!' I'm screaming … 'No … *no* … NO NOT THAT!'

A hand holds mine. We change rooms. Moments later I'm lying against his arm in the spare bed.

'It will hurt … you'll hurt me … I'm … sore,' I whisper, suddenly ashamed.

He takes my clothes from me. I feel awkward, scars showing plain on my body. I'm shaking uncontrollably. My eyes refuse to focus. But his hands are gentle, soft, not hard and dirty like Bill's. He doesn't want it for himself. He's giving it to me … a gift. I'm not in love with him or anything like that. I know this will never happen again. But just once, just once before I die, I'd like to know what it's really like to be held and 'loved' … and it doesn't hurt … his promise is good … after I feel like a woman … a real woman for the first time in my life.

* * * *

9 May 1975
It's as if I have a new purpose in my life. My step has a spring in it. I've broken the mindset of being a battered wife and leave Bill's dinner undone. *Who cares*? I'm concentrating on my own needs for a change, unwilling suddenly to let go of this woman I have become.

I wash my hair, have it cut and styled, buy new clothes with money put by for electric … oh, it's been too long! Bill can worry for a change about what to do when the red letter comes. Out in the world I wonder if I look different. Have I changed on the outside as much as I feel within? I try walking right out there in the sunshine near the kerb, instead of hugging the shadows of buildings. It's a time of new beginnings, new rules, brave new steps to beat depression.

* * * *

The next few months pass in what now represents normality in our marriage.

* * * *

Christmas Eve 1975
I sit alone, part of the party yet apart from it, a small glass of cider held in clammy hands. I'm trying to blend into the background. Music roars in my ears. Every so often, a fog mists my eyes and I feel like I'm going to faint. A fur coat brushes past me. A face peers into mine. The mouth is moving. Someone is speaking to me, but I can't hear. I smile back, turn away. A stabbing pain behind my eyes. I stifle a yawn. Almost midnight. When can we go home?

The music stops. It's as if suddenly I've gone deaf. People are holding their breath, waiting for that magic moment. Outside bells peal. A shout goes up. Everyone is kissing and hugging everyone else. I have never felt so alone in my life. Then, near the stage, I see Bill … he's in the arms of a blonde.

Colour Me with Hope

Where there is no vision, there is no hope

19 January 1976

Our second wedding anniversary. Not even chocolates this time. He just didn't remember. I'm drifting backwards into a deep dark place. Already my resolutions are part of the past. We're rowing over the little things, like Bill forgetting to get bread and cheese when he goes out and buys a new guitar instead. Or the fact I haven't made my last pound stretch to something special for tea.

23 January 1976

Bill returns home 1.30am. Whereabouts unknown. He went out early evening not saying where he was going.

27 January 1976

Bill doesn't go to work.

28 January 1976

Bill still doesn't go to work.

30 January 1976

Bill not at work again.

2 February 1976

I'm fed up with having electric guitars blaring until the early hours of the morning, and find a part-time job as a Doctor's Receptionist. It lasts exactly one month. I love the work. Even the filing I manage with enthusiasm and zest. The people are patient while I'm learning, but then later, they complain about an odour. I don't understand it myself. I have no sense of smell. It's a family trait. My father was born the same. All I know is that if I'm panicked or put under pressure there is this smell … it is the smell of fear! It's embarrassing. I image this alien smell wafting around me, setting me apart, making me different. It's lost me two jobs already – a part-time job in a shop and a four-day stint in a cash and carry. Now it's losing me a third.

My new employer, a doctor, would understand, or so I thought. I explain how it happens only when I'm nervous, on edge, over-excited. He prescribes pills to take … Amplex tablets, two a day … for the rest of my life? Then quietly he asks me to leave. I add the pills to my collection, and plan my next move.

11 February 1976

Doctor's appointment. I decide to discuss my being asked to leave my receptionist job with him. However, he had a discussion of his own that he wants to pursue. Instead of the usual prescription for anti-depressants, he starts asking questions. Personal questions.

'I've been meaning to ask you for some time, is everything all right at home – between you and your husband, I mean?'

'Yes, yes of course. Why?'

I can't tell him about my private hell. I can't even admit it to myself just how bad it is, and that I'm being beaten. I'm too close to the problem and refuse to let go the dream that everything will turn out fine … somehow … some day soon. Without Hope there is absolutely nothing at all.

'There is one thing, though …' I add hesitantly. 'Is there anything wrong with me? When Bill comes near me I freeze. I find it difficult to communicate, to come together. He thinks I'm deliberately blocking his advances. I don't. It just hurts.'

There's an awkward silence. I shuffle uncomfortably in the chair, beginning to wish I hadn't said anything at all. But then again, I want to know. I have to know if it really is my fault. The worry about being frigid, not having children, being afraid of sex, it's eating me up inside. Besides, sex has become a central theme in our marriage, a massive bone of contention between Bill and myself.

The previous week we'd tried to make love. Bill was sober for a change and I was determined to succeed. I forced myself on through the inhibiting act of undressing, cowering down at the side of the bed to slip shyly out of my clothes. Then the painful point of penetration when suddenly, I seemed to dry up. I'm left naked, screaming with pain. The more he forces, the more I tense, panic, cry, scream … the worse it is.

'I'm trying, really I am Bill. It just won't go.'

Bill doesn't believe in foreplay. What is foreplay anyway? To me it's a word, unfamiliar, mentioned in magazines read in a Doctor's waiting room. It doesn't belong in real life. At least, not mine. He barges straight in, thrusting forward … ramming, ramming, ramming … battling against the invisible barrier within which prevents him entry.

'Open up, you bitch!'

A slap sent my head jolting to one side. He seemed to think this was done on purpose.

'Spread! Come on … spread those legs!'

I'd known then how this session would end … and I was so right. He forced my legs apart. The watch on his wrist left a long red scratch on my flesh. It felt sore. My hand came away from my face with blood on it. I'd bitten my lip.

Bedclothes were snatched from the bed. The centre of the action changed to the floor. It was hard. My back hurt. He took hold of my breasts, pushing them round and round in a rough kind of caress. His nails dug in. He didn't seem to notice, didn't seem to care. All he wanted was sex, any which way he could.

'Come on, you little bugger. Get in.' He was breathing heavy.

'Please Bill. Can we stop now?'

'Stop? We've hardly bloody started.'

'But Bill … it just won't go in.'

He pushed harder … *ramming, ramming, ramming …
hurting … hurting … hurting.* He left my breasts and
moved his hands down to my sides. They clamped
down on one of my bruises. I leapt at least two inches
into the air, screaming in agony. Still he kept *ramming,
ramming, ramming,* determined to have his way no
matter what. He was a man deranged.

'I'm sorry, I'm sorry,' I sobbed.

I was always sorry, taking on board the guilt. It was
always my fault. Finally, he threw me with force
against the wall, and walked out. Didn't come home
until the following morning. Didn't say where he'd
been. My punishment was only ten pounds
housekeeping. My dilemma was which of the seven
outstanding bills, fines, HPs did I pay a little towards,
which ones to leave.

The doctor was speaking, gathering instruments
together, pointing to the couch.

'Oh, you don't have to do anything. I just want
advice.'

I'm not certain what he intends, but I have a suspicion it
will hurt. I'm still very sore, very raw and aching, and I
don't want him to see bruises.

He insists.

'I promise I'll be gentle.'

I've never had an internal. It isn't pleasant. I keep jumping, tensing, moving involuntarily so that the whole thing takes a lot longer than it should. I hear him catch his breath and look quickly away. My face is hot with embarrassment. I'm sure he's seen a bruise.

'But my dear, my dear, you're a mass of infection. No wonder it hurts!'

He prescribes pills, more pills, different pills. As well as infection, I've a condition known as '*Vaginismus*'. It means that my vaginal muscles tense involuntarily, closing together to become an impenetrable wall. It means, even if I'm not rejecting Bill, my body certainly is. 'If you can't protect me,' it's saying, 'then I'm going to have to protect myself.'

The doctor lends me a book on the subject to read at my leisure. But I'm seething. I'm so angry, so mad with myself ... *with him*. I mean to hit Bill right between the eyes with this. There are other tests I need to undergo, and it's plain that I'm the wronged party in all this. I spend the bus ride home piecing together what I will say.

Suddenly, it's not my fault any more!

But my words are never said. Bill is in a foul temper. He's a lot on his mind – a finance company is threatening to take him to court. He's debating doing his usual trick of borrowing a hundred from another source to pay back this one. Robbing Peter to pay Paul ... but then what? I keep my thoughts to myself and begin preparing the evening meal.

144

It's raining. He's not going to work. Not even my new ploy of putting joke items in his packed lunch, coaxing him like a child going to school, will make him change his mind. It worked at first – liquorice, kid's sweets, rubber pencils, imitation pencils, they all enticed him to the factory, curious what his lunch box might contain. Everything he does seems to be a game ... at least to him. It's as if he's still learning, still growing up. Right now, his toy soldiers are spread across the floor. He's staging a mock battle and refuses to be interrupted. This could go on for hours. I keep his dinner warm and eat mine alone in the kitchen. His will probably still be there tomorrow. We're on short rations this week and he hates making do.

'Why don't we ever have steaks?'

'How ... on the money you give me?'

'Well, other women get the same as you and don't complain. Twenty-seven quid is a lot of money.'

I sigh heavily, knowing we're heading for an argument I just can't win. I repeat the age old refrain: 'But they probably don't have court fines, HP payments, finance loans, all on top of gas, electric and rent.'

27 February 1976
Bill brings home just £17 wages for the week.

12 March 1976
Bill buys himself a new bass guitar.

20 March 1976

The doctor keeps in touch. He wants to see Bill on his own, probably to teach him about the finer points of passion. But Bill isn't playing ball.

'It's you there's something wrong with, not me … I always said it was you, and now I've been proved right, as always.'

He is blameless. Of course he is! He's not going to listen to a word I say. Never mind the infection. And foreplay? What's that? Just holding back the inevitable … so why bother? And my feelings? Love? Hey, what planet did I jump off from? These words are foreign to him. I'm his property, to do with as he pleases. He turns the stereo up to blasting point and closes his ears to my words.

26 April 1976

The supermarket is crowded. It's an age to get there and I want to get down the list as quick as possible. Hot, humid, stuffy, arms brush past me sticky with sweat. I need a new pair of tights. Mine look old and laddered in too many places. I stop to envy a lady across the way who appears fresh-faced, friendly, appealing.

Tins of peaches are on offer. I put two in the basket and cross off toilet rolls from the list. We can make do another week. I head for the till. There's a queue. My left leg is hurting where the latest bruise is coming up a vivid shade of blue. I shift uncomfortably from one foot to the other. The girl in front moves away. I heave my heavy basket up onto the rack, wasting no time in putting the items into my bag, keeping a careful eye on the till roll to see I haven't gone over my limit. A sigh of relief escapes me as the till tots up the amount.

'Six pounds, eighty-seven pence, please.'

The cashier is harassed, impatient to see the end of the queue and take a break. The lady behind is already pushing to take my place. I reach into my purse … and freeze!

It's empty!

'Come on, come on … I haven't got all day, you know!'

I'm dazed, shocked, silent, still. Everything is happening in slow motion. My thoughts are numbed. My feelings blanked. I can hardly breathe.

'Please God, please let me be wrong', I pray as I open and shut my purse, as if by some miracle money will appear, and I can pay the bill.

Nothing!

I start to take items out my bag, stammering apologies.

'There's been a mistake,' I mutter.

'You bet there has!'

The cashier is furious. A supervisor is sent for, but the shop is just too busy to cope.

'I left my purse behind,' says I, still trying to justify the situation.

'But you have it right there in your hands, lady. You think I'm stupid, or what?'

'Oh, you don't understand.'

I'm close to tears, trying desperately to hold my emotions in check. Customers behind want to get on. They're complaining about the delay, while I'm still fiddling nervously with the edge of the tins, rolling them round and round, in their labels looking for answers. A supervisor seems impossible to find.

'Look, I can't spend any more time on you. There are other customers waiting to be served,' the cashier scribbles frantically on the till roll.

'What shall I do?'

'You'll need to put all the items back into a wire basket, and go around the shop with it replacing them, won't you?

With a withering look she dismisses me, and I shrink to two inches high.

It takes a long time, and those who haven't heard what has gone before, look at me oddly as I put items back on the shelves. I dither with the packet of tights. I feel even worse than I had when I came in. I won't be coming back here in a hurry. A pair of eyes are watching me from the next aisle – a store detective? I replace the final packet and hurry out the store and home.

'… but how could you do that to me? It was so embarrassing …' I rave at Bill later.

He shrugs, it didn't happen to him, what does he care? The volume of the stereo is turned up full blast. An easy way out when he doesn't want to hear.

'What did you do with my money?' I'm shouting to make myself heard.

'Your money? Who the hell earns it? Who works his butt off for it? How can you possibly call it *your* money … when it's mine … all mine. You're lucky to get anything at all.'

He slams off the stereo and storms out. Moments later, I hear his latest possession judder into life. The green van needs an MOT. Bill has an out-of-date provisional licence from his motorcycle days. He doesn't have insurance or tax. I know if he gets caught who is going to bear the brunt.

May 1976
Sex or lack of it means shouting, arguments, misery. Alopecia for Bill means moods flaring up and his head having bald patches amidst his otherwise thick wiry red hair. Tension doesn't help my periods at this time of the month. I'm told it will be easier after we have a child.

I'm embarking on a different course of action. Employers and employment bureax aren't interested in giving me work when they see how tense and shaky I am. So I'm trying for small part-time jobs … four hot sweaty days in a fish and chip shop with the owner reaching to grope below the counter; Avon cosmetics, a foot slogging exercise; guitar lessons, one hour each week to four different pupils at one pound a time. Anything to raise a few pounds. I'm trying to believe I'm saving funds to leave him for a new life.

Jean Rich, my friend next door, has just had a baby boy and wants to start work as a barmaid. She's willing to pay me half her wages to look after the child while she works. She's had her problems – a husband goes with other women. We often sit and share our troubles over a coffee at her place.

I answer an advert in the local paper for home envelope-addressing, receiving by return a list of firms who are interested. I start at the top and work down. But all they send after six weeks of waiting is a parcel containing one thousand yellow leaflets for distribution. *One thousand*! It seems I have to post these through allotted doors … and there will be no payment. Only when this is done can I move on to 'bigger and better' employment. The accompanying letter calls it an initiation test to replace the usual interview. When my worthiness and dedication have been proved, I will be sent details of how to begin my envelop-addressing in earnest. It doesn't make sense. I spend a couple of weeks trying to locate the elusive company concerned, then I ditch the leaflets in the bin.

While I continue to answer adverts for childminders and contact Social Services about home-help work, Bill and I lead separate lives. Weekends I spend alone.

Weekdays I work at making the budget eke out. And I eat … eating is a substitute for love. Now when money disappears from my purse there are chocolates in compensation. I eat them anyway. His idea is that any extra money I bring in means he can help himself. We don't talk any more. My words, my voice, Me … they irritate him. He prefers the company of Hot Ayr and the ceaseless round of records, booze and fags.

7 June 1976
Bill not at work.

10 June 1976
Bill spends £30 wages, I don't know what on.

12 June 1976
Discover he's behind on HPs and court action is threatened.

17 June 1976
Bill not at work because it's raining!

19 June 1976
In arrears with rent as well as HP.

27 June 1976
It's a stormy night. Our rowing continues through until the early hours.

'This is it, Bill. I'm leaving. I've had enough. I've been lying to myself for long enough … it's over!'

He doesn't believe me. I hardly believe it myself. I've said it too many times before … and I've learned it's important that if you make a threat you have to carry it through.

'Okay, I'll help you pack.'

He grabs a suitcase from the top of the wardrobe and begins filling it with clothes. It stuns me for moments. He really means it.

However, the effort of packing a suitcase seems all too much for him, and he shuffles off to bed. But I know he expects to find me gone when he wakes. I stare down at the suitcase for a long long time. Then manhandle it down the stairs and out through the front door. I catch the early morning bus for Birmingham.

My parents are staggered to see me on their front doorstep.

'Cherub, what a wonderful surprise. Lovely to see you …'

I feel all warm and gooey inside … so welcomed … so loved. But they think it's an ordinary visit. They talk about everyday things … their everyday things like washing and shopping, meeting friends, lunches out. My sisters are discussing their futures, the way it will be, who they will be sharing it with. It isn't my world. How can I tell them? Why don't they know? I thought it would be so obvious from the way I am, the way I look. The doctor picked it up ... why not them?

I catch the next bus home.

Bill is asleep when I tiptoe through the door and make tea. He's been asleep all day and remains unaware that I ever really left at all.

July 1976

His body bears down on mine ... pounding, pushing, pummelling, pinning me to the bed. He is swearing softly, crudely, as he shifts position. I can feel bones through flesh. Long nails that need cutting scratch my legs. Glazed eyes stare vacant into mine. It isn't me he's doing this with but the girl in his dreams. I feel used, second hand, cheap, something nasty he's picked up from the gutter. He calls it 'making love', but nothing is further from the truth.

It is rape. Cold-blooded, calculated rape.

I hate myself for putting up with it as fingers find a hold. I gasp at the onrush of pain. It crashes over me, like waves towards a shore. My mind screams for a return to sanity. I become demented, deranged, temporarily insane. My body wriggles and writhes, crying out to be left alone. But he holds me fast. There is no mercy in him. He will get his due.

'Bill. Let me be. Let me go. Leave me in peace,'

My words fall on deaf ears. If anything, the pace slows. Things are not going well. This is always my

*point of dread. It only makes a bad situation worse,
and extends the whole proceedings. I try to accept
things the way they are, to lie back and think of
anything but the here and now. Sometimes it works.
But then the beery breath and the bristles
scratching my cheek bring me back with a
vengeance to the present.*

*My left hand moves to the side to get a grip on the
pillow. A pair of scissors lying on the dressing table
slip to the floor. Bill's regular writhing movements
never falters as I reach down after them. I clutch
the cold steel. It gives me courage to do what I have
to do. Then and only then can I be free ... free from
oppression, guilt, despair. Free to live and laugh
and love again. Free simply to be Me. It's the only
way.*

*I drive the points home with all the anger, the
venom, the fury that is in me, built up over years of
abuse. A look of surprise is etched across his face
before pain takes over. His body falls limp and
heavy ... smothering ... claustrophobic ... across
my own. I'm shaking, in shock I guess, living again
the memory of that last fatal moment.*

Then I'm awake … It's all just a bad bad dream.

A footfall on the stair. Muttering. Cursing. The
bedroom door bangs open wide.

'Hiya … how's about a bit of nooky?'

It isn't so much a question as a statement. My dream is about to become reality, at least in part. He has come to claim what he believes is rightfully his.

He stumbles into the room. Drunk. A hand jerks his belt undone, fumbling with the zip. It catches on his pants, and he pulls them angrily apart. There's a ripping sound. He steps free of his clothes to bare his bony body. The bed creaks and groans in protest. I try desperately to turn away, to be brave, to refuse the advances ... but too late!

He is clawing at my nightdress. For the first time I glimpse the half finished fag between his nicotine stained fingers. A smouldering cigarette end can be lethal in the wrong hands. I know it already to my cost. He loves the idea of fire play, taunting, tantalising, teasing, and already my hair has been singed to the point it grows thinner on the left side of my head. My left nipple is inverted. The hair on pussy is less, and the skin around the vagina lips sensitive.

Now he launches into a full blown attack. I pray it won't take long. My body, still sore with infection, aches for a reprieve. I want to scream and shout, to strike out at the enemy. Instead, I lie tense and still, awaiting the inevitable.

He presses down on me, exhaling the breath from my body. I feel suffocated, gasping in agony, light headed, sick, weakened. A pair of scissors lies on the dressing table, tantalising me to the point of distraction ... and I remember the dream. But they remain so far away ... out of reach ... and the rape continues on.

He comes to the point where he can go no further. My body won't let him in. The impenetrable wall shuts him out as an alien. For moments he lies back, breathless and spent. But the worst is yet to come. He makes me do things I don't want to do … acts that sicken and repulse … kneeling in front of his frustrated body, a hand holding my hair tight, painfully dragging my head down into his hair as he pushes his penis inside my mouth. I gag and vomit, swallowing the sick, retching, pulling my head back, having it forcibly shunted back into position.

'Come on, bitch … make me cum.'

The thought of it is enough. I pull sharply away, leaving some of my hair in his hands. He grabs my face, forcing my mouth open, jerking me down like before.

'Come on, come on, come on …'

He pushes my head down and up, down and up, down and up, in time with his words. Suddenly, his body is rigid. He is pulling me up to his torso, gripping my hair savagely, forcing me to lick him from top to toe.

Finally, it is over for another night … another week … if I'm lucky, another month.

*   *   *   *

Later that same night we are calling the police to report a burglary. The equipment belonging to Hot Ayr is stored downstairs in a lock-up and Bill's amp has been stolen. Strange that the thief would take only one item when there is far more expensive gear on offer. The police obviously think so too. I say nothing. I'm remembering that Bill is behind on payments and the letter he received the other day from the company concerned giving him seven days to pay, or else. The amp is never seen again.

11 August 1976
Bill refuses my request for £10 more per month to pay bills and keep out of arrears.

17 August 1976
Beginning of weekly appointments with the doctor. On tranx due to strain at home and money worries.

31 August 1976
3 months behind with payments to Bill's tailor.

September 1976
Another year of marriage is drawing to a close. Nothing is changing for the better. Bill seems more than ever like a little boy, with a constant need for games, mock battles with his toy soldiers. At times it's like he's trying to push me to see how far I'll go. He stays out late, comes home drunk, often now he can't get up of a morning for work.

He brings home in wages ten pounds or less having spent most of it on sweets, fags and booze. I'm lucky if I see a couple of pounds to live on. Any bills or ominous red letters that arrive he stashes away unopened in a drawer, as if they'll somehow go away of

157

their own accord. And he's forever complaining about meals.

'Eggs again ... but we've had them twice this week already!'

'And you've got them again tomorrow. You're lucky to have a meal at all with the money you bring in.'

'You go out and get a job then. I feel shut in ... caged ... an animal trapped ... and it shouldn't be this way. Marriage did that to me ... marriage ... and you! You've chained me like a prisoner and I hate, hate, hate, HATE IT!

The bit about me getting a job struck home. I'm always answering adverts, being turned down when I arrive at interviews shaking. I can't hold a cup and saucer without using both hands. But now ... well, okay ... I'll show him!

I arrive at a plush hotel and feel dowdy. It doesn't help to be greeted by the glamour girl behind the desk.

'Can I help you?' She looks like she stepped off the front cover of *Vogue*. I wilt into the wallpaper.

'I'm here for an interview? For the job of receptionist?'

She looks like she stepped on something ikky in the street.

'Sit over there and you will be called, Mrs … Miss …?

'Mrs D…., thank you.'

But instead of moving to the chair, I walk on out the door. This isn't a place for me. I'd bring down the tone. The girl calls after me. I break into a run. And I don't stop running until I step on the bus that will take me home.

I stay a little longer at the next interview. It's another receptionist job, this time at a small surgery. I spent money put by for the gas on a new £12 coat. At least it hides what I'm wearing underneath.

'Can you do a specimen of your handwriting?'

Pleasantries over, they move quickly on to business.

'And have you a reference? Why did you leave your last place of employment?'

My hand starts shaking. My writing streaks across the page like a spider inspecting his web. Every word is an effort. The pen is thin and small. I've difficulty holding it never mind trying to hold my hand steady and the writing neat and in the line. The office is stuffy. My stomach is turning somersaults, wondering whether the dreaded smell has returned with the fear. I wish I hadn't come.

'Well, thank you for coming, Mrs … We'll be in touch if we need you.'

A word, a nod, an official handshake, it's over. I am dismissed. They aren't waiting for explanations or a chat. They've already made up their minds.

Two and three times a week now I mention to Bill I'm leaving, packing my bags to start a new life on my own. But then where can I go? I'm still desperately afraid of being alone, of having no-one to look after and come home to. I'm afraid of having only myself to think of, of giving up my husband, my home, the life I have now ... despite being so awful and being so helpless, it's the only life I have.

I'm scared to stay ... scared to leave. What can I do?

Encouraged by Jean Rich's husband, Jeff, I start jogging sessions at six every morning. Running gets rid of my rage. It leaves me feeling limp, tired, with no energy for feeling and emotion. Yet at the same time I experience exhilaration, excitement. I am aroused by it.

Together, Jeff and I slog slowly, tediously, exhaustedly around the park and end up on a bench for a chat before crawling home. One morning, two policemen are there to meet me as I circuit the field for the fourth time. A woman who lives in a house overlooking the park has telephoned them.

'Now then, Miss. You're quite safe now.'

'Eh?'

'Yes, we'll deal with him.'

'Deal with who?'

Jeff arrives on the scene at that moment.

'Okay. If you'd like to accompany us down to the station, young man.'

'What is all this?'

Jeff is indignant. I'm too puffed to say or think anything. But the police are only too willing to explain.

'We received a phone call to the effect that there is a young man chasing a young lady through the trees in the park. We are here to offer assistance.'

It would have been funny if it wasn't so serious.

Jeff is constantly offering to drive me away from Bill and the beatings to my parents in Birmingham. He's concerned. He and Jean listen through the wafer-thin walls of the maisonette. He and I on these morning walks talk about my life, and for a short while after, I'm left feeling encouraged, happy with my dreams of what could be for the future … until reality kicks in.

I sing at Old Age Pensioners' Clubs, schools, hospitals, churches. I write concerts on a theme of faith, hope, love.

'Love between two people can be a very happy and wonderful thing,' I'd preach to the converted, as if I had a wealth of experience behind me.

After, they'd shake my hand, thank me for coming.

'You're obviously a lucky girl, and a very happy one, very much in love with life, and your husband, he must be so proud of you ...'

I live my dreams through my songs, and it's almost a psychic shock to be jolted back into the present and have to return home.

September 1976
One evening I return home just ahead of Bill, still euphoric. It has been one of my best performances. I've sung until my voice is hoarse, finishing with a medley of 1930s hits which I love so much. Still singing '*A Nightingale Sang in Berkley Square*' I flick the switch for the kettle, and Bill rolls in. *Where has he got the money to buy drink this early?* It's suspicious, but he's in no mood to be questioned. I should be used to seeing him drunk, but then, this is something else again. He's almost paralytic.

'Get outta my way, bitch.'

He pushes me roughly aside, and makes for the sink. Missing his target, he's sick all over the kitchen floor. Vomit clots on the lino. My mood quickly changes from anger to disgust. I want to puke myself, and it's me who will need to clear up the mess.

'Ah, that's berra!' He offers a long low burp. 'Now, gotta have a pee ...'

I suddenly wonder what he has in mind. I've never seen him so drunk. I'm scared. The stairs are bearing the full flood of the waters, puddles smudging the carpet, spraying the walls.

'Bill ... ' I'm screaming, half panic, half ... I don't know. '*Not there!*'

'*Where then, where then?*' he mimicks my tone.

I try pulling him up the stairs, over the puddles trickling down. It occurs to me how easy it would be to simply push him down the other way. To push him down the stairs ... and run. He evades my grasp and heads back to the kitchen.

'For heaven's sake, Bill ...' I agonise, seeing him reach up to spill a stream of beery urine into the pans of veg and meat on the cooker. I am sickened at what we've become. How did we reach this low? I try pulling him away, dragging at his trousers dangling around his knees. I want to take hold of his penis and yank ... *hard.* I know it's the only place I can strike back. He will take it as a threat to his manhood. But equally I'm certain he will kill me for it. He'd have no way of stopping or holding back in the state he's in now.

It's useless. I'm not sure if he's deliberately egging me on, goading me in his usual way, or if he really is too drunk to know or care where the bathroom is. Then he starts to climb the stairs, teetering off balance halfway up. I push him the rest of the way from behind.

'*Leave he alone,*' he yells. '*Leave me alone.*'

A hefty shove from behind sends me reeling. I lose my footing and fall back down into the hallway. My head is swimming, my left arm hurts. A bump the size of a golf ball is rising rapidly on my leg. Every part of me aches. I climb up onto the landing with an effort. Bill is sprawled on the double bed. He's passed out. A cigarette smoulders on the bedclothes. I pick it up and throw it out the window … I could happily throw myself I feel so wretched. Then I'm stepping gingerly back down the stairs, gagging at the stink, heading next door for sympathy. Jeff is livid. He wants to go straight round to punch Bill where it can hurt and do most damage, but I won't let him. It will only make matters worse.

Next morning, Bill can't remember a thing. He has a raging headache and swears I'm making it all up just to get at him. I wish I'd left the mess just the way it was.

Later, I discover my pregnancy test is positive … *oh joy! I am ecstatic*!! I've been putting on weight for weeks, despite all my jogging and dieting. My doctor had asked me to give in a sample at the Women's Hospital, and these are the findings. Despite my longings for a child, my hopes that a child will change Bill, when faced with reality I'm no longer so sure it will solve anything at all.

One question: *what if he hits the baby as well as me?* My work in Children's Homes has taught me enough to be aware of the psychological effect caused by environment on a child.

Another question: *how will we manage financially?* I'll never forgive him if I can't provide a proper home and if my child becomes deprived.

My doubts lessen as I break the news. He's delighted, over the moon, kissing and hugging me, leaving for work singing.

'Oh Jan, you've made me so happy! You've made me so proud. You'll see, I'll make it all up to you.'

I want to believe, I want to believe so much.

And yes, things change. Over the next few weeks, he works overtime, paying off outstanding bills. He even acquires a weekend job as barman at a pub down the road. I have his company in the evenings when he isn't playing with Hot Ayr, and he's kind, gentle, thoughtful. It's like having a new man. I'm no longer allowed to carry cumbersome shopping, and every chore he does with a smile. My hopes have been rewarded ... *thank you God*! Happy ever afters are really going to happen.

18 October 1976
Bills now in arrears £58.62.

4 November 1976
Car insurance in arrears and action threatened.

13 December 1976
He takes £5 from my purse, although he knows it isn't my money, but collected from Avon orders.

22 December 1976

I find a payment card for a new guitar and case.

Life Can Be a Dark and Lonely Place

This is the true nature of home
– it is the place of peace, the shelter,
not only from all injury, but from all terror,
doubt and division,
a sacred place, a temple of the hearth

John Ruskin

5 January 1977

Dear Mum and Dad,

It was lovely being with you all at Christmas and thank you for all you did to make it so happy.

I begin babysitting again this weekend for Jean and will be glad of my new hobby of knitting toys, especially if Bill decides to go out and I am home alone. I too dream of what it would be like if we lived nearer, perhaps in the same street; and could share a cup of coffee and do our shopping together. In the lonely evenings it would be particularly appreciable and we could take it in turns to keep one another company.

But these are just dreams and at least I have a new venture to occupy my time. It does seem rather appropriate at the beginning of a new year!

The months ahead will no doubt bring many changes, as well as good times and bad. However, with our preparations for our fist child I now have things to plan for. I realise only too well it won't be a bed of roses and I shall get moody and depressed some days. Also, it is likely to prove difficult with Bill working nights, and having to cope on my own much of the time.

I have a positive ache for a baby to hold at times. I know I have enough love to offer him several times over. I just hope I can gather together some of the material things he will need over the next twelve months. Of course, there is also our holiday to Yarmouth with you that I am very much looking forward to and I need to save as much as I can towards it. Bill now has three part-time jobs – he had a lot of debts to pay. But don't worry ...

We saw the New Year in at the Carousel Club singing Auld Lang Syne on stage with Hot Ayr. It was a moment to remember. Afterwards, everyone began kissing everyone else which went on for a good half hour. We eventually crawled into bed around three in the morning.

Come and have tea with us on our anniversary if you can. Make a day of it. It would be lovely to have someone to share it with.

Looking forward to seeing you soon,
Janine

27 January 1977

My pregnancy … my phantom pregnancy … lasts three months.

The doctor commiserates:

'If you want something badly enough, sometimes you can begin to make it happen.'

All the signs, the symptoms were there. I was sick in the mornings. The sight and smell of tea and coffee repelled me. I grew in size, and could even boast a little hump. But there just isn't any baby there.

I feel so empty. My body aches for the child that isn't to be. My whole being cries out with loss. Within the week Bill has reverted back to his old ways. I'm alone with my sweet dreams.

Loneliness is like a disease. It eats away at the human heart until there is nothing left. I hardly see Bill now. I'm on edge, careful to keep out his way, fearful of every move, every word, lest I upset him. Money, bills, the future, myself, are all taboo subjects. They irritate, antagonise, and lead to arguments which in turn end in beatings. It is as if the last few weeks never happened. Loneliness breeds discontentment. Discontentment breeds hate. And hate can destroy a person's will to live.

For three months I'd been happy. Now, once more, all I have for company are broken promises and lies. We live like strangers. *Why do I stay to take more of this undeserved punishment?* I stay because I would not, I could not go. Something inside me … pride or foolishness … prevents me taking that final step.

5 February 1977
Doors bang. Chairs scrape. Voices chatter. Teacups rattle in saucers. People begin to take their places.

'Can I have your attention, please …?'

The Over Sixties Club shuffles into seats. The concert is about to begin.

'This afternoon, ladies and gentlemen, I have great pleasure in welcoming a very dear friend of ours. She needs no introduction I'm sure, and without more ado I shall pass the meeting over to … Mrs D.'

I look reprovingly in the Speaker's direction.

'Janine, please,' I murmur, as spontaneous clapping breaks out, filling the hall with sound.

My cheeks are burning. My body is sweating. The bruise on my leg begins to throb. I fiddle with the music stand, shuffle papers to give my hands something to do.

'I'll wait until you're all quiet …' I begin, struggling to secure the guitar strap around my shoulder, my arm is hurting so much.

'*Shush … shush …*' an agitated front row whisper around the hall.

170

'I'm very pleased to be with you all again,' my voice shakes a little. My throat is dry.

'For those who don't know me, my name is Janine, and this afternoon I bring you my own brand of humour and music. Not pop. Not folk. But songs written by me especially for you.'

Stomach cramps begin to ease. Fingers find the chord of E major. I strum jauntily into the first song:

> *'Love is everything that money cannot buy,*
> *It begins with the simple things in life.*
> *Love can make you sing,*
> *Love can make bells ring,*
> *Love is everything ... everything to me ... '*

My voice rings with conviction. No-one listening couldn't fail to know it's true. Faces beam up at me. I smile back ... confident ... sure.

'What are your favourite words? Can you tell me the words that you most like to hear?' I fix a lady in the second row with a quizzical stare.

'Apple pie,' comes an amused voice from the back.

Laughter ripples around the hall. Others take his cue.

'Spotted Dick!' shouts another. 'Nobody makes Spotted Dick like my muvva used to make!'

'Coronation Street!' adds a third.

A couple sitting at the back start a shaky rendering of the theme music.

'No … no … no …' I sigh exaggeratedly, as if I'm running out of patience.

'*I love you,*' I shout, crisp and clear.

'*And we love you too,*' comes the response.

I launch into my next number, a wobbly smile playing around my lips. I feel choked. My leg hurts like crazy. My bruised thigh has become numb.

> '*Love stands for care and honesty,*
> *All of the good things that we'd like to be.*
> *Love is to be loved and loved in return …*
> *Caring, sharing, trust and concern …*'

My breaths are almost sobs. I'm gulping air as if there's no tomorrow, trying desperately to gain my composure.

'Now … what does the word '*Love*' conjure up? Two people. Engagements. Flashing diamonds, perhaps?'

If only … if only …

'Candlelit dinners, holding hands, laughing, loving? But then look what happens? You get married and there are always dishes to wash, baths to clean, floors to scrub, dinner to do. Chores. Never-ending chores. What becomes of all those romantic ideas of yester-year? Where do all those tender moments go? Down the plug hole along with the dirty bath water?'

I'm trying to keep my voice light, bantering, kidding along with them.

'Well, my next song is dedicated to all you hard-working housewives out there …'

> *'Get back to the kitchen, Woman,*
> *Get back where you belong.*
> *It's not your place to play a guitar,*
> *To write, to sing a song.*
> *You're just a woman,*
> *One of the weaker sex.*
> *Your place is the kitchen*
> *To wipe, to clear the mess.'*

Bill's words.

> *'Woman, what're you doing?*
> *I want my dinner soon.*
> *Get on with the cooking*
> *And don't ask for the moon.*
> *Woman, I don't want to know*
> *About the price of food.*
> *You're the one who buys it*
> *And well … I'm not in the mood.'*

Everyone loves it … it's written all over their faces … some are even trying to sing along …

> *'Pick up your dish mop, pick up your bowl,*
> *Pick up your dishes too.*
> *This is your place, and you must keep pace,*
> *While I finish the Pools.*
> *But don't get any ideas*
> *About picking up a book.*
> *Get back to the kitchen, Woman,*
> *You've got my dinner to cook!'*

173

Thunderous applause. People laughing, clapping, standing in appreciation of a good song, a skit on the average housewife. I'm physically exhausted. Mentally drained. My head is pounding. My bruised leg throbs. My mind is numb. This is my life I'm singing about, my life they're applauding, and they don't even know.

'Thank you, thank you, thank you everyone.'

Shakily I walk to the side of the stage, grasping a pile of tatty papers. Everyone is still, quiet, expectant.

'I was having a spring clean the other day, like you do. You know, you wake up of a morning and think, well, today's the day kiddo! It has to be today 'cause it just won't wait any more. Dusters, mops, polish, hoover all come out the cupboard. But then, hello, what's these right at the back out of sight?'

I blow the top of the pile, watching with satisfaction the cloud of dust-cum-flour liberally sprinkled a couple of hours beforehand flying up into the air. I blow again for effect. People laugh as I pull at a sheet yellowed with age, carefully opening it out:

'*News of the World*,' I read slow and clear, '*April 28th 1940*.'

There are a few gasps on the front row. People shuffle forward in their seats, intent on the sheet I'm holding in my hand.

'Now then ... let's see ...,' I rustle the papers, running a finger along the column heading: '*Missing*

174

from Home.' 'Call *for Women.'* 'What *War is Costing Us.'*

'Ah … here it is. It says: '*Whisky will be increasing to 16s a bottle, Gin to 15s 6d a bottle.'*

The hall is so quiet I can hear the uncomfortable wheeze of the gentleman in the third row from the back, and it's a large hall!

'*Cigarettes will cost* 8½d *for 10 and to post a letter you will now have to pay* 2½d *... Ah, those were the days.'*

A murmur of agreement whispers along the rows of listeners. This was always the kind of thing they liked to hear.

'The following is a preciously preserved extract from a love letter written to his wife at home by a soldier on active service: 'Don't send me no more nagging letters, Letty. They don't do me no good. I'm many miles away from home, and I want to enjoy this war in peace.'

Clapping … talking … tears …

'And now, in the words of Semprini … *some old ones, new ones, loved ones, neglected ones ...'*

I sit at the piano praying it's going to be in tune. There's nothing like a scattering of notes when they're off key! I've a pile of 1938 songs ready. I choose one at random and listen for the well known tune to catch on. More follows. '*A Nightingale Sang in Berkley Square,*

175

Down at the Old Bull and Bush, Carolina Moon, If You Were the Only Girl in the World. Tears flow unashamedly down my face. I think back to the moment I was watching the old black and white movie on TV, when Bill first came knocking on our door. How different this might have been. This is the real Me ... not the cowed submissive slave I am at home.

'We must finish soon, it's almost four,' a voice whispers urgently in my ear.

I bring the concert to a close.

> *'We'll meet again*
> *Don't know where, don't know when.*
> *But I know we'll meet again*
> *Some sunny day ...'*

Strains of the old familiar melody follow the people out the door.

'Mrs D ... Janine?'

A lady I remember vaguely from the sea of faces approaches me, and I turn to grasp her outstretched hand.

'I just want to thank you ... to thank you for such a lovely afternoon. I loved that song *'Get Back to the Kitchen, Woman'*. You must have a very happy life to write like that and be so in love with your husband. You're very lucky, you know.'

I'm avoiding her eyes, pushing music into a bag, stuffing guitar in a case.

176

'Anyway, thank you … thank you. Rarely have I spent such a pleasant afternoon.'

She disappears into the crowd, and I grab my bits and pieces and leave by the back door.

Give Me Wings to Fly

*In our vulnerability we can sometimes find
the strength we need to survive*

7 February 1977
My first real brutal attack from which I sustain injuries.
What has gone before fades in comparison.

It's a cold, wet Monday. Bill has been out with Hot
Ayr. Returning for tea unexpectedly already he is
complaining bitterly. I'm washing dishes in the kitchen.

'What, no tea made for me?'

'I wasn't expecting you. You didn't say what time
you'd be back.'

'And the gas is out. What did you let it go out for?
Do I have to do everything around here?'

He bends down to light it, and I lay a warning hand on
his arm.

'Watch out for your cigarette.'

He shakes his arm free.

'I know, I know, I know. You think I'm stupid, or what? Get back to the sink, woman. Maybe you'll get around to making me something to eat eventually.'

The sneer is in his voice, unmistakable. It's a dire warning that he's reaching for an argument.

'Please Bill, I've just started with a period. I don't feel well at all. Leave me alone.'

It's a red rag to a bull! He charges full pelt … coming at me with all the venom and fury that has been building up in him. *Maybe it's me not doing my wifely duties. Is it the whine that has entered my voice? Maybe he would have done it anyway.* His right arm lashes out like a whip. I catch the full force on my cheek. It stings. I taste blood. I'm feeling sick. The sting stays with me as I try to leave the room. I want out, before it gets any worse. But he's blocking the doorway with his frame.

'Stop acting like a swine and let me go … *now*!'

Oh, brave words. *But stupid stupid girl!*

His right arm is already moving. It slashes my face, hits my jaw … *hard*. I hear it make contact like the crack of a whip as I bite my tongue. My hand reaches up to massage my jaw back into place.

'Bill …'

My tongue is a blockage in my throat.

'Bill … Bill will you stop it … please?'

I'm trying every tactic I know … appeal … anger … finally escape. But there is no place to run when violence is happening in your own home.

The bread knife sits on the draining board. As a last desperate attempt to keep him away from me I take hold of the handle, moving it between us, threatening … thrusting menacingly each time he attempts to come near.

'Keep away, Bill. I warn you. I'll use it.'

He backs off then and I try edging around him and on out the door. But he isn't that frightened. He isn't going to let me by. He starts towards me. I have to do something. I don't have the courage to use the knife on him. He knows it. And so I turn the knife on myself.

Surprise!

I close my eyes for a split second, praying for the strength to do what I must, reminding myself that a threat doesn't mean anything if you're not prepared to carry it through. When I open them, he's like a snake ready to strike. I can't hold him much longer.

My hand grips the handle and I drive the blade towards my belly. He uncoils, springing at me like a tiger from a corner of the room. All hell breaks loose. His fingers tighten around my neck … squeezing … suffocating … I drop the knife, hearing it clatter on the floor. There's the sticky feel of blood in the palm of my hand. I try to keep my face covered as I hit the floor. The kitchen tiles come up to greet me … and …

180

everything is a blur … there's suddenly a lot of space around me before I pass out.

I come to in a rain of kicks … he's kicking me, stomping on me, over and over again. Feet jab viciously in soft flesh. His face looks evil. Never has he looked so ugly, so menacing, so full of rage. This is my husband. The realisation hits me as if for the first time.

My husband?

Pain doesn't register at first. I feel numb. It's like I'm sitting on the very edge of a precipice waiting for something to happen. Dragging myself up onto wobbly legs I try to wipe away the blur that has become my world and head towards where the door should be. It's at the far end of a long dark tunnel, and takes an age to reach it. The living room … a sofa … I cling on tight.

He appears out of the mist and starts over, using me like a punchbag. My arm is weak and useless as it rises and flops back to my side in an effort to fend him off. Then I'm sliding to the floor.

I don't know how long I'm unconscious. But when I come to I'm at the back of the sofa. Peering around the edge, Bill is sitting comfortable with a bottle of beer and a bag of chips, watching a comedy on TV. He's relaxed, happy, actually smiling.

How can he be that way after what's just happened?

My mind stalls. I slide back to the floor and wait until he leaves for work. He doesn't even look my way, just bangs out of the flat in his usual fashion … the slamming of the door sounding like a thunderous roar, reverberating round and round my head for a long long time.

8 February 1977
His first words the next morning to me:

'God, you look a mess!'

I daren't look in the mirror. It's enough to be told. Swollen bruises colour my right side. My hip hurts like crazy when I walk. All I can see of my stomach are large black and blue blobs. Both shoulders ache incessantly from being slammed against the wall. My head hurts, and a blinding headache develops quickly into a migraine bringing spots before my eyes. As well as anti-depressants, I take two painkillers every four hours for the next few days.

I sleep in the spare bedroom and refuse to budge from the flat until my injuries have healed. It's embarrassing. I feel too much of a failure to consult my doctor for help.

13 February 1977
Takes Avon money from my purse.

11 March 1977
We have a routine. Bill sleeps all day, getting up in time for a meal before going on nightshift. He practises with Hot Ayr every Saturday, then plays out on gigs

with them until one or two the following morning. Sunday is spent at a friend's house working on the car.

28 April 1977
Bill takes the night off work due to car running out of petrol. He's still driving with a provisional licence.

5 May 1977
Bill takes night off work.

16 May 1977
Bill changes to a dayshift in an effort to leave me on my own less.

26 May 1977
Bill has taken money from my purse. He's also spent the money Hot Ayr gave him to give to me for the HP I'm paying on their behalf.

1 June 1977
Bill spends the group's money again instead of giving it to me to pay. Now in arrears.

2 June 1977
I discover he has taken Avon money again and spent it. Now trying to hide Avon and catalogue monies. This evening we try to have sex for the first time in several months.

20 June 1977

Bill takes day off work to see about buying a new car.

21 June 1977

Bill off work again.

30 June 1977

Bill disappears after tea, not saying where he's going. Arrives home after midnight after I've spent the evening ringing round trying to locate him.

14 July 1977

Bill disappears late afternoon. Arrives home midnight.

23 July 1977

Holidays … at last! After months of worry and waiting I'm pleased to be able to give my parents a holiday shared. I'm trying to put out of my mind the money it has meant borrowing from the bank. I can't put out my mind though the large white Zephyr bought by Bill. He simply drove home one morning in it instead of the green van he'd been using … said absolutely nothing at all.

'I haven't seen that car before around here, have you?' I comment at breakfast, more to create conversation than anything real interest.

'Er … yes, as a matter of fact … it's mine.'

He continues eating as if it were an everyday occurrence for him to buy a car.

'But how … I mean, where did the money come from?

I'm feeling sick to the pit of my stomach, somehow dreading the answer.

'Money, money, money, that's all you think about. You tight-fisted Bitch! We've got it, that's all.'

He storms up to bed, while I hurry to check the savings. They're all gone from the hiding place, every last penny. Almost £200 set aside for the holiday, and it has taken me so long to save from what little he gives me. Bank and Post Office Savings Books are too easy for him to check. And so I left them in a place I know he knew. That way he'd check the balance and be satisfied that was all we had. But then it meant keeping money in the house, always dodgy. Now we have nothing, only money put by for bills … and my Avon collections.

'You fucking bastard!' I scream, tears streaming down my face.

I'm just so angry, I don't care any more. I feel like I'm going to burst with emotion. But it's wasted on him. He lies smoking in bed, a sardonic smile on his face. It's done, sorted, he'll take the grief. But nothing is going to change what's done. It only makes me feel worse. I'm at a complete loss how to hurt him in the same way. It never does work the other way around. Maybe I just don't know him as well as he knows me.

Yarmouth … it's packed with people … heaving at the seams. Music from the amusement arcades carries on long into the night. Not the ideal place for a holiday, or to bring my parents. And it rains. The weather matches my mood.

The guest house has an electric organ, so for at least a short time I'm able to lose myself in my music, while the clamour and confusion carries on around me. I feel I've let my parents down. This isn't what they would have chosen. They deserve so much better. I also realise suddenly why Bill has so readily agreed to a foursome. We hardly see him. He's up early, off to places he wants to go … Stock Car Racing, Snetterton, rallies …. My parents are along for the ride, and to keep me company.

24 July 1977

'I'm just going for some fags before turning in. Won't be five minutes.'

'I'll come with you.' I'm longing to link hands and walk along the prom as I've seen other couples do.

'No, you stay here.'

He slips out like a shadow. I don't even see which way he goes.

My parents and I retire to bed at nine. It's been a tiring day. He's been gone three hours, but I keep thinking I can hear him, creeping like a thief in the night, same as when he comes from work to home. He's probably gone to the pub for a quick one.

By midnight I'm worried. I keep getting up to check the window. But there's no sign. I debate about going out to look for him. But I'm scared about going out alone at night. I read for a while without concentrating, having to start the page over, and then over again. Everyone has retired to bed, even the owners. This is going to be embarrassing. I creep along the landing and, after a moment's hesitation, knock softly on the door of Room 4. Muttering and scuffling within, then Dad edges open the door. When he sees my blotched face and wringing hands he tugs me in and we hold a hurried family conference.

'It's two in the morning, for crying out loud! Where has the lad gone?'

'Oh, he isn't being fair on the girl. Look how worried and upset she is!'

They show mixed feelings as I stand, crestfallen, looking down at the carpet like a naughty schoolgirl who has just been found out. He's always disappearing, coming home without a word of explanation or an apology. I can't tell them that.

'Has he ever done this kind of thing before?'

As always, Mum is right there on the ball.

'Well … yes.'

I'm afraid to admit the truth.

'There you are then. He'll come back when he's good and ready.'

187

I couldn't stop the various possibilities flashing through my mind. He'd fallen off the jetty and been drowned? Mugged by a roving gang and lying fatally injured somewhere? Dad sensed the way my thoughts were working.

'Look Poppet, if it will make things easier, I'll go out and call the police if he's not back in half an hour.'

Half an hour goes by like it's days. Dad begins to dress. I let loose a fresh flood of tears. I feel so awful … so awkward … the proverbial schoolgirl …

Outside feet scuffle past the door. I peep through the crack. Bill's receding figure slopes past.

'He's back!' I announce like it's the new day's headlines.

'Right,' mutters Dad. 'We'll have this out here and now as to where he's been until three in the morning. What does he think he's playing at?'

I had an idea he'd enjoy Bill's excuses. But Mum interjected.

'No Darling. Leave them to sort it out.'

As always, she believed it wrong to intervene between husband and wife. *Was she right? Should she have allowed Dad to have his say?* Right then I'd like to have seen Bill squirm.

Back in the bedroom he's retired for the night, just as if nothing is wrong. The light is out. He's pretending to be asleep. I prod him to make sure.

'Bill ... Bill where have you been?'

It is a question that remains unanswered to this day.

4 August 1977
Spend day in town after being unexpectedly awakened by Bill. Very randy and loving. He keeps tantalising me despite my pushing him away. We come together to achieve almost heaven. It's difficult. It takes time. But it's the best for a long long while.

I think we both feel different after. We spend the morning cuddling and kissing. Something very new for both of us. It makes me feel all warm and loved inside. Even the loss of my Avon collections over the weekend fades into insignificance. We blow some housekeeping on a cheesecake and éclair to celebrate. The evening is ours watching TV together.

It really has been the best of days, and it feels good suddenly to be alive.

11 August 1977
Bill takes money from my purse and turns violent when I challenge him. My fits of dizziness and shaking return.

19 August 1977
Bill disappears.

We're watching TV after tea. I turn round to speak to him and suddenly, he just isn't there any more. I assume he's upstairs. But after half an hour he hasn't appeared, and I go to look. His jacket is gone from the hall. It seems he's slipped out and vanished into the night.

It reminds me of those times in the bedsit. I'd finish washing up and return to his room to find him gone. Just like that! I'd spend hours worrying myself sick, staying on until he returns, needing to know he's okay. I have to see him back safe and sound before I can sleep. It's as if he's a wayward son and I his mother.

He rolls in drunk at two thirty … but I've heard his approach long before he reaches the front door.

'*Shhhh* … ' I whisper, peering out into the blackness. 'Be quiet or you'll wake the neighbours.'

'DAMN THE NEIGHBOURS!' he yells as loud as he possibly can. 'They're all too bloody nosey, anyway.'

He bangs the door too hard, shattering the lower pane of glass. Automatically, I'm right there, sweeping up the mess, terrified of what Bill might do in the mood he's in if let loose with one of the jagged edges.

'I've been out having a drink with me Dad,' he boasts arrogantly, daring me to challenge.

'… and he agrees with me, I should have more money for myself in future.'

190

Oh God! I try to keep calm, composed, rational, it's important not to show he's rattled and upset me. I won't be drawn into an argument ... not now. But we have one anyway. He hits me across the face, shouting I'm a tight-fisted, money-pinching cunt. All I can think is that the neighbours can hear every word coming from the twisted snarling lips of my abuser.

'Please ... please Bill, please be quiet?'

'Sod you! I don't have to do what you say.'

'Bill ... please ...'

'HEY,' he shouts at the top of his voice. '*If you really want to know what's going on, come and take a peek at this ...*'

He flicks his wrist, catching me a glancing blow by my eye.

'Stop it, Bill,' I scream.

He laughs. It's a game ... his game. He knows the rules. He's the champion. Playfully, he punches me hard in the stomach, then punches me again with all the force of his body behind it. I fall heavily. His foot buffets my side. I try crawling away. But he's kicking savagely into my body again ... and again ... and again ... and again ... then he's running off into the night.

I sit in the kitchen alone contemplating the bottles of pills.

What's the point of going on? Things are never going to change. I hear the door being pushed open, and flinch, my arm already above my head, protecting ... he's back already? But it's Jean from next door. She's been wakened by the noise and worried for me. She sits until four when he returns ... sober. Not a word is said. He stomps upstairs to bed. Jean leaves, taking all my tablets with her. I feel naked, helpless without them.

26 August 1977
The end of a very depressing week. I've fallen for that old ploy, when Bill has borrowed money on behalf of his father. Fifteen pounds we've loaned him to tide him over while he's in 'financial difficulties'. He's collapsed at work, a heart attack they're calling it. When I last saw him he looks old and grey.

I phone to ask how he is. They thank me for the loan.

'We were glad to be able to pay it back with interest,' his stepmother tells me.

When had they paid it back? Later I ask Bill. He's already spent it. On precisely what, he can't remember. Or he won't say.

Just before our holiday, we made friends with Kate. She lives in a ground floor maisonette below us. Jean, next door, has her doubts about the friendship. She's heard rumours about Kate, nasty rumours, she believes come from a reliable source. Jean warns me:

'Be careful, Jan. She's a dangerous person to know.'

192

Kate's answer to the accusation is:

'I make a bad enemy, but a very good friend.'

Things have been going well between us. She buys items from my catalogue, and I buy from hers. We shop together in town, and I see less of Jean and more of Kate. Then everything starts to go wrong. Nothing I can actually put my finger on, just suspicions. Money disappears from my purse which was on the table in her kitchen while I was upstairs. But then again, Bill has been there too – who is to blame?

The same happens when rent money disappears. Bill and I go down to ask her to pay ours along with her own. I put a note on her table with the rent book, we have a coffee and chat before leaving. But then, as we're going out the door, Kate turns to me and says:

'Where's the money then?'

'I put it with the rent book on the table.'

We're already in the street outside when she rushes after us.

'There's no money there.'

We traipse back to see if it's slipped to the floor somehow. But it's gone. Again, Kate … or Bill … or Kate … or Bill?

When we go on holiday, she agrees to look after things for us. We give her the key. But on our return, £27 I'd hidden for bills has gone missing. Did Bill find it? Or is it Kate who's taken it? Always there's that element of doubt. Now she's helping with a Council exchange. There's a friend of hers who wants a maisonette. She has a house a distance away. I can't wait. The chance of a new start, new beginning, and the house has a garden back and front.

28 August 1977

We move into our new house. It's a dream come true. For the first time I can look out the window and see green grass ... never mind it needs cutting, full of weeds, in urgent need of restoration and flowers ... it's a place I can hang washing with our very own dustbin. It's the little things that make it home.

2 September 1977

Dear Mum and Dad,

At last, I've managed to find time to write. It's the first chance I've had this week to even sit down and relax for half an hour or so.

We really are thrilled with our new home. Today, I spent an exciting morning hanging out our washing for the first time ever. Now we have almost all the rooms straight it looks so cosy – just like a dream come true. Then I look out the window and see our garden, a little overgrown perhaps, surrounded by a hedge, and I find it hard to believe it's ours.

We stepped through the door on our first day here and Bill said 'Put the kettle on, Love. We're home.' It sounded good. We are home. The future suddenly looks so much brighter and I even have two neighbours. Two new friends. It was only when we had anyone staying with us at the maisonette that it ever seemed to have any atmosphere. All the rows we had when we were alone convinced us that it might not only be us but the place in which we were living.

Bill takes such a new kind of pride in our new house. In fact, he has taken to shaving twice a day and wants a clean shirt and trousers every morning. I am still on my own most nights, but he does bring me home a little surprise sometimes, some present he thought I might like.

Well, I really must stop my chatter and get on with some work. There is definitely no shortage of jobs around the house. Yesterday I almost broke my back laying carpets. Bill had disappeared as usual. Now I have backache as well as a big plaster over the end of my thumb where I spliced nearly all the fingernail off with a Stanley knife after hitting it first with a hammer. I wish Bill had been around to help more ...

Over days that follow, I try to ignore blocked drains, an overgrown garden littered with rubbish, grimy windows, the at times overpowering smell, and the little red spots beginning to cover our arms and legs. It dawns on me finally ... *we have fleas!* Perhaps this isn't the slice of heaven I'd dreamed it to be. I scrub, disinfect, scrub again, clean the house from top to bottom. I've begun taking two baths a day I feel so unclean and contaminated. Now we know why the couple, Kate's friends, were so keen to move when they did.

6 September 1977
I haven't heard from Kate since we moved and I'm wondering about her catalogue payments. I paid my debts before leaving the maisonette. But she still owes £50 on goods she received through me. I decide to pay her a visit.

7 September 1977
Paul, Kate's husband, arrives early saying she has thrown him out. For the first time I'm uneasy. While bill is talking about putting Paul up for a few nights in the spare room, I run to catch the first of two buses it will take to get to their home.

'What are you doing here?' Not quite the reaction I expected.

'Look Kate, all I'm interested in is the money you owe me for the catalogue.'

'I don't owe you a penny … but then you owe me £40.'

I'm stunned.

'But I paid you it all in full before I left. You know that.'

'Prove it!'

Her two daughters make a captive audience. It's true she omitted to sign my catalogue card. I have no proof. I trusted her as a friend.

'Please Kate, stop messing about. Give me the money and I'll go.'

'Now look, you pathetic little creature. You're a real innocent. I took you for the sucker you are, and just you try to prove I owe you money. If you dare take it further I shall claim I never received the goods.'

I'm all the things she says ... that's the worst part ... and she knows it.

'And furthermore, I shall deny ever accepting payments from you. My catalogue will be getting in touch about the £40 you owe.'

Suddenly she's a witch, a woman to beware of, everything Jean and others warned. She asks her eldest daughter to get Louise, her friend. I just want to go, to leave this house of lies. I'm crying. I feel so betrayed. Now I'm blaming myself for all that's happened ... typical! But I can't move, I can't run, I can't get out the door. My body refuses to function.

Kate is still talking. I hear but I can't make any sense. Suddenly, her words filter through. She's saying Bill and Paul threatened her at knife point, that they robbed the meters and took her money ... *No!* But she goes on and on and on with her accusations ... and my feet take flight ... I'm running for the door ... I can't get away fast enough.

'Where do you think you're going?'

Louise, the woman with whom we exchanged houses, stands in the doorway. I've been set up! No mistake. I try to push past. Through a blur of tears I see her smile. It's the same sadistic smile Bill always has, as if enjoying my plight, getting a buzz out of my pain.

'*Let me go, let me go,* '

Someone is screaming. I think that someone is me!

Kate pulls back and slaps my face hard.

'Did you see that?' I gasp at our audience, her two daughters giggling in a corner.

'She never touched you,' they answer almost in unison. Puppets on a string.

It's a conspiracy. *Is this really happening ... to me?* Kate slaps and punches, punches and slaps, until I feel blood welling up inside my mouth. As they step back, I run right out the door. On up the stairs I run to Jean's, feeling the hounds baying at my heels. Surely Jean won't let me down? She has always been my friend. But then, what is a friend? I'm not certain any more who to trust ... who to believe.

Jean opens the door, helps me inside, pours me hot sweet tea, calls a taxi. Then I'm home ... *home*? I retell my tale of woe to Bill and to Paul, Kate's husband. It's Paul who calls the police.

'Do you wish to prefer charges?' the young fresh faced constable asks kindly, after looking at the damage to the inside of my mouth, the mis-alignment of my jaw. He looks sideways at Bill.

'You're sure your husband didn't do this to you?'

I smile ruefully.

'I'm sure. And yes, I want to press charges.'

Talking hurts. My lower jaw is displaced. I have a cut on the inside of my mouth, three chipped front teeth. But the irony doesn't escape me. I've been beaten up by a woman and I'm prosecuting … while for all these years … nine in total … I've been beaten by Bill and never done a thing!

8 September 1977

The solicitor makes it all sound so petty. To make matters worse, Kate's daughter still has my guitar I lent her. I'm told now there's no hope of retrieving it, even though I can prove it is mine.

'These domestic disputes just aren't worth fighting,' he says with a sad shake of his head.

'Believe me when I say you are best leaving well alone. You can both end up being bound over to keep the peace.'

'But surely, she can't just be allowed to get away with it?'

This is now about proving something to myself as much as to the law.

'Please, Mrs D.... Allow me to know my job. I'm telling you to pursue this matter will cost money, time and effort. My advice is to leave it alone. However, she will receive a police warning, if that is any consolation.'

It isn't any consolation at all! But then again, he's the expert. What do I know? I leave his office and head for the doctor. I'm shaking from head to toe in the waiting room. Every part of me is on edge. He gives me more tablets together with ominous words:

'You are about to know the difference between Depression and Acute Depression. You are suffering from shock, young lady, and I advise you to go straight home to bed and to take a sleeping pill. Come back and see me in a few days.'

10 September 1977
My sister Laura's wedding.

The ceremony makes me cry. Please God, let her marriage be a happy one. Let her never know the shame of being beaten or betrayed. The buffet looks so lovely. I watch from afar, my jaw still too painful to let me eat. They leave in a hired car for a honeymoon in Dorset. Suddenly all my own worries crowd in on me again, and I begin to cry ...

I could have predicted what Mum would say:

'You silly girl!'

Dad is furious. He asks me to stay on with them for a while. A break sounds good ... I should have stayed longer.

14 September 1977

Dearest Mum and Dad,

Thanks for putting up with me. Today is grey and miserable. It matches my mood. The minute I walked through the door on Monday evening I felt like turning round and coming right back again. Dirty dishes overflowed in the sink. A pan, black and burned, had been put on top of the fridge leaving an imprint. The bedroom looks like a bomb has hit it. Bill saved no money for me, and I'm having to borrow fifty pence for bus fare to get to my doctor's appointment ...

I feel as if the whole wide world is against me. I want to shut myself away and never surface again. The smallest job demands too much effort. In the end, I stop answering the doorbell or go downstairs. I lie in bed, caught between sleeping and waking. The pills stop me thinking, stop me hurting inside. The only post which comes is from Kate's catalogue, informing me I've been put on their 'black list', demanding I pay them £40 to avoid court action. Dad replies on my behalf. They write the same again. The thought of a court hearing hangs over me, making me sweat and shake with fear.

I remain nervy and on edge. A woman answering Kate's description has called while I was away. Now I hate being alone in the house, I dread what will happen next.

'Please Bill, stay with me tonight. I'm so afraid.'

'It's boring being in,' and he's off out to play with the band. Often he's paid £50 for a performance, but I see none of it. What he spends it on I have no idea. The following day it's gone and he'll come begging for more.

I lie in bed listening to the traffic, to children going and coming from school, the milkman on his rounds, the evening rush hour traffic. The house is a tip. It just isn't home any more. And I don't care. Nobody cares, why the hell should I? Bill has only to speak to me now and I'm in tears. He takes what he wants from my purse, and when it's empty, he knows there is no more.

21 September 1977
Bill in arrears with a loan I didn't even know he had.

22 September 1977
Bill spends all money due to be paid out next week.

26 September 1977
Another course of tranx from the doctor, literally being sick with worry. Start weekly appointments again.

28 September 1977
Bill stays off work. No money for bus fare.

3 October 1977

Today marks the beginning of recovery. It began when I heard a small child crying bitterly outside the window.

'Mummy, Mummy, where are you?'

It came to me through a fog of despair. It was a cry very much like my own. If only it didn't mean failure in a fragile world. He thought he had beaten me and won. I wasn't done yet. But then, in making that cry my own, who was going to answer ... who was going to help? Who was actually going to be there for me?

No-one.

I drag myself out of bed, sit by the window, looking out on a desperate world, crawling with evil, uninviting. I could so easily drag the bedcovers back over me. But then, there's that cry. It is my own. To face the world is my challenge ... my Everest. If I don't help myself, no-one else will.

4 October 1977

I'm up, washing and brushing my teeth for the first time in weeks. It takes time to pick the pieces of my self up off the floor and stick them back together ... with Hope. It's all I have left.

From this day on, I do what I've done the day before but then add something new, something different. Okay, it's something other people take for granted. But this is little old me we're talking about. And I keep going on this level, upstairs, until the day I can face going down … to make my own breakfast in the kitchen.

Hallelujah!

I have arrived … somewhere!

'You're up then!' Even he is incredulous. It's like a small miracle has happened, and he's fast going to take advantage.

'Eh, haven't a pound or two you can lend me?'

Things are back to normal or very nearly … *but then again, are they?*

Weeks later and then some, my health isn't good. I suffer dizzy spells. My legs give way, making me sit down suddenly. Migraines fog my mind. Mum and Dad are worried. They make the trip from Birmingham almost every week to take me out for a while before bringing me back home.

They have no conception of what my life is like. I am too ashamed to tell them. I blame myself for everything that is wrong. Now Laura, my sister, is practical, sensible, dominant, assertive … all the things I am not … a daughter of whom to be proud. She and Ralph are buying a house. They have plans neatly packaged and tied up with string. I try to imagine me in her situation … can't be done! She would have left long ago, at the first hint of something wrong. Not stuck it out for almost ten long years … first as a battered girlfriend, then a battered wife.

So why me? Why am I all kinds of a fool? Why do I keep coming back for more?

6 October 1977

Bill brings home £9 for a week's wages. I wish I knew where the money goes.

10 October 1977

Doctor puts me on a stronger nerve tablet.

13 October 1977

Week's wages £10

5 November 1977

Bill takes all the money from my purse for a night out.

14 November 1977

A car pulls up outside the house. I don't recognise the man who is walking up the garden path. A debt collector? Another?

'Mrs D....? I'm afraid I have bad news. Shall we go inside?'

My legs collapse under me. A summons for bills in arrears? A bailiff? Worse?

'Your husband has had an accident at work. He's at the hospital now and in shock. They want to do an emergency op. I can take you there now, if you like?'

He has to steady me as we walk to the car. My head is reeling.

Bill looks shaky, pale. He takes my hand in his, holds it for a long time. He's smiling lopsidedly. He needs me. I adopt mother role. They have no idea what is wrong. I'm asking as they take him into surgery, and a Sister tries to explain but her words are fusing together.

When next I see him his hand is heavily bandaged, held upright in a splint. He's ground his finger instead of the piece of metal he was working on. He'll be off work at least a month. I daren't think of the consequences, not then. I'll simply pass out.

At home I take two sleeping pills … and withdraw quietly from the world.

15 November 1977
An ominous rap of knuckles on the front door. Two policemen are standing, looking very formal and official.

'Good morning. Is this the residence of William David D …?'

'Yes … yes that's right.'

Net curtains are twitching in the house opposite.

'May we speak to him please?'

'I'm sorry, he's not in. I mean, he's in hospital.'

The two exchange glances. I explain the situation.

    'Well, thank you, Mrs D....'

They begin to walk away.

    'Can I help?'

I'm only the wife, but at least I feel I should know what's wrong.

    'We want to see his driving papers. As you are probably aware, he was pulled up last week for having no tax and insurance. We'll call again.'

No, I didn't know. But then, what's new? I shut the door, wobble to a chair. And when I've stopped shaking enough to write, I make a list of what we owe. It comes to a staggering £908.21 ... and that's without this latest incident, or any other HPs or loans I'm not aware of.

16 November 1977
Bill comes home from hospital.

23 November 1977
The police come back ... fine of £40.

26 November 1977
A crumpled letter dated some weeks previous sits at the back of a drawer. It demands '*the balance of an outstanding loan taken out for a Ford Zephyr, registration number ... be paid in full within twenty eight days or action will follow.*' My mind jerks back to

the morning I commented on the car outside and found it to be his. Always, I had assumed the £200 that went missing from our savings at the time went on this. Now I can only boggle at what he might have bought with such a large sum.

1 December 1997
This is an errant boy I have for a husband, not a man … an unreliable, unfeeling, selfish boy to boot. After doing all the running around for both of us for money to survive while he's off work … Social Security Industrial Injuries Benefit, taking my place at the back of a very long queue, receiving a nod and a shrug in response … He doesn't care. He seems to have the impression life will right itself on its own … it generally does doesn't it?

I'm upset. I'm crying. All he can do is laugh. How can he be so callous, so cruel? Finally, he grabs the remainder of money in my purse, saying he's going to collect one day's wages he's owed from work. I'm due to sing in a concert. Now I don't even have the bus fare to get there. An ashtray is thrown in my direction leaving a vivid welt.

9 December 1977
Bill disappears for the day. Leaves home at 8am saying he won't be long. Arrives home at 10.30pm … row! Why am I pretending? How can I make believe it's true? We don't have a marriage. It's a farce. There is no connection between us … was there ever? So why do I stay? But then, where can I go if I leave? That's the eternal triangle … it is what holds me here. Nothing more.

20 December 1977

As a child, this was always my favourite time of year. I buck myself up now by decorating the house, cooking pies and cakes. But marzipan, mincemeat and marshmallows keep disappearing from the cupboard. Then chocolates from the tree ... the best ones shaped like Santa, with cream inside ... my favourites, it seems Bill's also.

I'd bought a hamper from the catalogue, paying it off steadily through the months. Now, lovingly almost, I undo the string, a moment I've long been waiting for, yearning to drool over the goodies and place them in the cupboard ready for the big day. My hand delves into the straw ... and comes up ... empty? Where is the food? I turn the carton over not able to believe it's true.

It's been opened from the bottom.

'Oh, that ... you found it then.' His reply is offhand. His don't care attitude infuriates me. I'm learning to answer back.

'I found it alright ... empty. What the hell did you do with all that food ... flog it?'

'No, as a matter of fact I ate it. I took a tin or two in to share with my mates at work. I owed them, okay? They lent me money and I needed something to fob them off cause they were coming back at me.'

What can I say? I can't bring it back. The deed is done. Over. Finished. Done. My nails dig painfully into the palm of my hand. I want so badly to let rip, to wipe that sardonic smile from his face. To smack and hit him the way he has me too often in the past. *Am I becoming him? Am I now no better?* His evil can be contagious … like measles … it will start to show.

I hate him more and feel more against him at this moment than I have ever felt towards another human being. It took so much effort on my part to get the hamper … all for nothing.

'What's the big deal, anyway? It's only food.'

I slam out the room, pound the stairs, pack my case.

'You're leaving then?

He stands at the door, smoking.

'Where will you go?'

He has the upper hand and he knows it. I think of my sisters … my parents preparing for Christmas mixing with church folk and all the good citizens of the Parish. Everyone has plans, especially at this time of year. I can't spoil it for them. I can't leave … not now.

My case remains packed. I pretend it's a warning … but hey, who am I kidding? I'm not even deceiving myself.

21 December 1977
We're at a party. The other three members of the band are here with their girlfriends. It's one of these boozy affairs where drink flows freely. I set out to enjoy myself, to create a 'what-the-hell' attitude. But then,

I'm sitting alone, listening to the girls talking about fashion, make-up, work. My interests are books, writing, photography, music. What have we in common? I feel so much older than my 24 years.

'And what have you been doing with yourself, Jan?'

The question comes in one of those awful silences. All eyes are on me. I'm blushing furiously. Bill laughs drunkenly. I feel like the butt of a joke I don't know anything about.

'Oh, nothing special,'

I try to answer as airily as I can, as though it doesn't matter, but my voice gives me away. It matters a whole bloody lot … it hurts like hell that I'm not making more of myself.

'Have another drink,' Johnny is leaning over, refilling my glass. His other arm is latched around Dee. They look so happy, looking forward to Christmas Day. I glance over at Bill, pouring liquor down his throat as if it's water.

Suddenly, I'm off the chair and running from the room. Hell, I don't even belong here. I'm not one of this crowd. I'm Me, only I haven't had the chance to properly find myself yet. All I really have are dreams.

'We'll have to be going,' I announce to the assembly on my return.

'Mummy says, does she?' Bill chants from the far corner as if it's a nursery rhyme. He's refusing to budge and I sit it out for another half hour. Then others begin to move and as Bill lurches forward, I see how drunk he really is as his glass smashes to the floor and he laughs inanely.

I'm scared.

'Please … can someone give me a lift home? I don't want to go home with Bill.'

There, I've said it. No holds barred. I just blurted it out … and it's followed by a stunned silence. No-one is moving now. It's like a film suddenly broken mid pace.

'Oh, come on … don't be so silly. He's your husband.'

'I know … and I don't want to go home with him.'

Yes, it sounds ludicrous. But do they really not know what he is really like? Do they really have no idea? He's not the only one worse for drink, but he's the only one capable of violence.

'You can both come with me,' Johnny offers. 'I'll drop you off at the chippy at the top of the road.'

I'm still not happy, but with the last bus gone a couple of hours ago I can't afford to say no.

The more we approach the road in which we live the more upset I become. I tell Bill he can go to the chip shop and I'll see him when he gets home. But he drags me along anyway, and for good measure, pushes me in front of him, like I'm a prisoner liable to flee. It's raining. The pavements are wet, I slip and sit down hard in a puddle.

'Oh, come on, Jan, gerrup can't you ... I'm gerring wet!'

He's acting as if it's all my fault. Maybe he didn't like being shown up in front of his mates, but now I'm crying. I'm so scared, every part of me is shaking. And the more I'm crying the madder he becomes. In the chip shop he starts swearing.

'Bill stop it! You're making a complete fool of yourself.'

He shouts all the louder and they serve us quickly so we will go. I follow, ashamed, embarrassed as he wobbles down the centre of the road, trying to follow the white lines. Cars hoot as they pass perilously close, swerving to avoid the ridiculous performance, headlamps spotlighting us like rabbits on the run.

At home he upsets his chip supper over the sofa, then sets fire to a chair with his cigarette. When drunk he needs watching carefully if an accident is to be prevented, yet he hates having me around.

'Get outta the way!'

I recede to a far corner, but then rush forward as a second cigarette sets a piece of carpet alight.

'Let's go to bed ... please?'

He lashes out and the usual session of violence begins. It's happened too many times for me to be surprised. And there's nothing I can do except ride it out until he drops. As I try to evade his grasp, it's as if he has a hundred tentacles. He reaches out to twist my arm painfully behind me, all the time thudding his knee into the small of my back. It makes me scream with the sheer agony of the moment. He's breaking my arm ...

'Bill ... for pity's sake!'

Pity? He has none. It's not his way. He maintains a monotonous *thud ... thud ... thud ...* I'm trying to twist away but his grip is too tight. And he laughs. I'm crying. Always, always it ends in tears.

My head is jerked back suddenly. He has hold of my hair. When he lets go without warning I fall in a heap to the floor. In the interval that follows he lights up a cigarette. I watch his eyes as they try to focus on the end of it. It takes several attempts to strike the match that finally lights it ... and then ...

Silence.

He's staring mutely at me. Smoking. Waiting. Watching for my next move. I daren't aggravate the situation.

I'm not speaking, not moving, but then carefully, I start getting up off the floor. It's like dealing with a dangerous animal. My knees knock together. My right arm, the one he's twisted, is numb. No feeling whatever. Pins and needles shoot up and down as circulation returns. I'm gasping, falling backwards,

214

knocking painfully against the fireplace surround. It catches my knee and shoulder. For moments I'm blinded by tears. And still we maintain a stony silence.

When I dare to look, Bill is laughing. I'm shaking from head to toe. My teeth are chattering. My head is throbbing mercilessly. My arms flop heavily at my side. I'm sapped of strength. Bill drops the cigarette he's holding, and in a drunken state has to bend right down to focus properly on the floor. I heave myself up and make a rush for the door ... and the stairs beyond to barricade the door in the spare bedroom.

'Happy Christmas,' I whisper, as I cuddle a teddy bear to keep warm.

'Happy Christmas ...'

The War is Over

I left you in April '78
To make a life of my own
I should have felt anger, I should have felt hate,
But all I cried for was Home

2 January 1978
Bill not at work because he'd have to walk. No buses on Bank Holiday.

8 January 1978
I'm living in a kind of limbo, no longer a part of the world around me. It's like a bubble … one of those I'd blow through a hoop as a child and watch rolling in a burst of rainbow colours high up into the sky … wondering what it would be like to fly.

Sitting in the back of the car I'm listening to the two in front, talking trivialities, trying to keep my homecoming a special occasion. The vehicle speeds on through busy streets back to home … and Bill. I try to keep my mind on what Laura and Ralph are saying and not think about the mess I might find awaiting me. It's been good, being away for a while. Birmingham offered sanctuary, a place to lick my wounds, to gather my loins, to take stock, before entering the fray.

I feel old, too old. I can't shake off this dreamlike state. It's the pills, I suppose. But the doctor said on my last visit:

'They're what's holding you together, my dear. Without them, you would be a mess. You'd simply fall apart and become a nervous wreck.'

We approach the outskirts of town. Laura and Ralph fall silent. My knees are shaking. My stomach is churning. We draw up outside the house. The white Zephyr has been driven off the road onto overgrown grass, away from prying eyes of the police. Bill still has no tax, no insurance, no licence to drive. He's incurred a further £40 fine just the week before. But the car remains his prize possession. He means to keep it, whatever the cost.

I can put off the moment no longer. Ralph is already unloading my luggage, and I see Bill's face peering from an upstairs window. He opens the front door as I hesitantly walk up the path, slowly re-entering my prison.

I force myself to ignore the mess. Dirty dishes hide the sink. The living room carpet is spotted with ash. I stop myself automatically bending to clean it. The bin is filled with chip papers, the bed upstairs grimy and unmade. He stinks, no longer bothering to bath when he comes home full of factory smells and sweat. I sit down on the edge of the bed and cry.

10 January 1978

There's a hollowness inside me once crammed full of feeling. I have no more tears. It's an effort to get up and face another day with the weeks stretching interminably through the darkest of tunnels. I have lost all hope.

The lady next door knocks. The milkman calls for payment. I don't answer, watching through a crack in the curtains. The minutes tick by while I sit reading last year's diary. And I make a pact with myself. This is going to be my year. Things are going to be different.

18 January 1978

It's the day before our fourth wedding anniversary. Bill doesn't go to work … does it really matter why? It's his fifth day off in three weeks and he's been warned if his absences continue then he'll face the sack. He shrugs his shoulders in the face of authority. What does he care?

'How can they expect me to go to work without money for fags or bus fare?'

As usual, his argument is totally irrational.

'What about the money from your last gig?'

I don't know why I even bother to ask.

'Oh that went ages ago.'

He no longer feels he has to justify. What he does with his money is his affair alone.

'But you only got it Saturday. Still, if you insist on staying at home, you needn't expect me to be here to cook for you.'

Never make a threat unless you're prepared to follow it through. Remember that, my girl. Otherwise it's an empty threat and it means absolutely nothing at all.

'Where are you going?'

'Around.'

I'm trying to adopt an I don't care attitude. He hates that. But then he does it all the time! I'm coming round to the conclusion he likes to see me worried, crying, caring. And yes, inside I'm all those things and more. But just not on the outside where it shows. He can't see inside my head. I know that. I have to protect my feelings, to keep them safe.

I put on my coat.

'What time will you be back?'

'Depends,' I remain off hand, non-commital, uncooperative even, and I decide on the spur of the moment to dress up as if I really am going somewhere special without him. That would make a change, be something completely different to the Norm. So now he's edgy, worried. It's like playing a game of chess with him on the defensive … for once.

'Checkmate,' I mutter as I slam the door behind me and run for the bus.

I sit huddled over a cup of cold coffee, reassessing the Situations Vacant. Outside looks bleak and uninviting. Snowflakes fall on people rushing by. I'm putting off the moment when I'll have to join them in the cold. Then my eyes are drawn to an advert:

Receptionist wanted
for busy Hairdressing Salon in centre of town

I read the small print again, excitement welling up inside me. This has to be it! Please God, let it be?

I start walking fast towards the bus, but on impulse divert to a small boutique boasting a closing down sale. I spend a long time trying on, choosing what to buy. Finally I settle on a new coat and skirt with matching blouse, so different from my usual style. I pay for them using the gas bill money and, pleased with my purchases, head for home.

Bill is out. I'm glad. I don't want him seeing my new clothes. As I sit down with pen and paper I realise he's tidied up before he left. But I resist the urge to dwell on this rare occurrence. I no longer have any misconceptions about what it could mean. Bill needs money.

I post my letter and arrive back at the same time as Bill. He is carrying a battered guitar case. No, I'm not going to ask. His face shows he's in an evil mood. I escape upstairs to change, but he comes after me. He's obsessed with needing money.

'They wouldn't buy my old guitar, not even in a secondhand shop. I'm desperate Jan. I really really am.

Just give me a pound or two? Come on, you can afford it.'

'I'd like to, Bill, but I haven't more than 50p myself.

I carefully don't look towards the second to top drawer in the dresser which contains the remainder of the gas bill money.

'Where did you go, anyway?'

He hates not knowing, but I'm not going to tell him, not until I get the job, anyway.

'I had business in town to attend to,' I say importantly.

He starts then, shaking me by the shoulders. His nails dig deep into my flesh. My head rocks back and forth, to and fro. My teeth are chattering. My jaw aches. I feel like I'm being snapped in two. He pushes me down, drags me across the floor. The disobedient servant *will* bow before her Master …

'You animal! Keep off me, keep right away. You won't get a penny.'

'Bitch!'

His hand stings my cheek. The blow jolts my head back and I wriggle away from under him, slapping him as hard as I'm able across the face with the flat of my hand, trying to bring him to some kind of sanity and sense. I'm angry now. It's been a hell of a long time coming. But I'm angry as hell … angry more at myself for letting him treat me all these years this way.

Enough!

'Keep away, you brute. You're not getting anything from me.'

It's as if my secret is giving me power and the strength to rise up and resist. I make for the door, but he's too quick. He always was. The side of his face is red, his pride, his masculinity badly dented. He hasn't got it all his way this time. He grabs hold of my legs in a rugby tackle probably learned during his brief stay in the RAF.

'Go away … go away … go away!'

It sounds stupid and feeble, like a child's pitiful cry. Why can't I think of any of the suitable hurtful phrases he uses on me? I'm sobbing, gagging for air which I can't get in my lungs fast enough.

'Get away from me, you pig, you animal … you fucking bloody bastard. Fuck off!'

I missor his own language back at him and kick him in the chest. There's just time for a moment's satisfaction. He gasps. I've hurt him. *Wow*! But then he pulls my feet from under me and I crash to the floor.

'I'll fucking beat your hide for that, you little bitch.'

Arms wind around me like rope, crushing me, pinning me to the floor. I can't move. I've difficulty getting my breath. My chest is heaving with the weight, my head swimming. Blackness threatens to engulf me. I'm rapidly sinking into oblivion. Maybe I should let it ... let the blackness drown me and take me over. I try to get my arm free ... natural instinct, I guess ... he's holding it in a vice. My teeth sink into his wrist. It's the only way to be free.

'You little wildcat, you bitch! You'll pay for that.'

Fists hammer my head. The room hurtles around me. My head is a football against the side of the wall. All the time he stays just out of reach and then ... then he let's me go ... finally ... abruptly, before I can get my breath ... he's running from the house ...

Gone!

Slowly the merry-go-round in my head stops revolving. The head pains, dizziness and headaches stay with me ... lasting days. When I try to comb my hair there are painful bumps on my scalp. I hurt all over. But I can't tell the doctor. I'm still too ashamed of being beaten, of allowing it to happen. In the past well meaning friends have advised me to hit back ...

'Don't just sit there and take it. Hit the bastard, and harder, where it hurts him most.'

Now I've done that and I wear the scars to prove it. He's never beaten me so brutally, so cruelly. The scars are going to be with me for a very long time to come ... a reminder of this day.

A lesson learned.

2 February 1978

Bill is bouncing cheques in desperation. Some stupid bank gave him a cheque book and an account. He gains another fine for driving without tax or a licence or insurance, this time for £80. He's another £100 loan from a naïve finance company to get a bigger better amp. Daily reminders plop through the letterbox about previous court fines, HP arrears, loan payments. And there's a note about a bounced cheque to Readers Digest for a record.

But then … good news … *I've got the job*!

I'd almost ducked out at the last moment. Fifty candidates applied, and the six who sat buffing painted nails when I arrived for the interview looked cool, composed, confident, more than capable of holding down the job. I took my place in the queue and listened to a blue-eyed blonde boasting of her past experience.

'Of course, I know only too well the kind of person they'll be after. It isn't everyone who can do this work, you know. It takes drive, initiative, enthusiasm, a tidy mind …'

Her name was called next. She clip-clopped into the office, only to emerge a few minutes later, her bright red lips firm. Without another word, she passed us and was gone. A heavy silence fell over the remaining few. One by one we were ushered into the inner sanctum … one by one we left.

'You have to become part of a team. Would you mind if we re-modelled, re-shaped, re-vamped the outer you?' they asked when it was my turn.

'No, I don't mind at all. I want a change anyway.' The only thing I did stipulate was that I didn't want my hair dyed.

The salary was good ... excellent, in fact. They wanted someone with no preconceived ideas about the job. I would be looking after the books, and it might mean staying on after the others had left to balance them correctly.

'Are you prepared to do overtime,'

'Yes, of course.'

It would give me an excuse not to return home until Bill had left for work.

I'd been bubbling over with enthusiasm, wanting to tell Bill ... I had to tell someone ... to know they were pleased for me. But there was a film on TV. I gave up trying to compete. It pricked my bubble, made me feel deflated. He did buy me a small tin of spaghetti for a celebration supper, but I would have liked it a whole lot better if he'd given me a little more attention and said '*Well Done!*'

14 February 1978
The first morning of my new job. Valentine's Day. No cards, not even one from Bill. But then, what did I expect? Never expect, then you can't be disappointed. Lesson two learned. Suddenly, there's so much to do, oodles to learn, I flounder in a complete fog.

22 February 1978
Bill still hasn't paid the court fines despite him telling me he has.

27 February 1978
Dear Mum and Dad,

This is the first chance I have really had of writing you a newsy letter. Things have been very hectic this last couple of weeks.

Our day begins at six. It's awful to hear the alarm; and know that Time is the Master. Breakfast is a mug of tea, and a slice of toast, then Bill leaves for work at seven. I now have to spend a full half hour solely on make-up and nails, after a rather embarrassing demo at Boots. Everyone was leering at me while I was being painted. It is so much more trouble than my usual splash of cream and coat of powder.

I am usually the first to arrive at the Salon. There are customer bills to be made in readiness, telephone calls to answer, and pages and pages of bookwork. The bosses seem to have a mania for wanting to know how many trims, cut and blow drys, perms and colours each assistant has completed in a day. A system for doing this was devised by the boss's son who is slowly taking over the business, but it needs constant checks and re-checks. My head is reeling by the end of the day, and my feet feel like two blocks of lead.

28 February 1978

Bill keeps hitting me when we try unsuccessfully to have sex.

March 1978

It was fine at first me working. Then arguments flare at home.

'Where's my shirt for tonight? I need a clean one to wear on stage.'

'I'm sorry, love. I haven't had time to do it,' I can't rid myself of the overpowering tiredness I feel at night.

But Bill has no sympathy.

'Oh, come on, get off your butt and do some work. You don't know the meaning of the word. My job is twice as gruelling as yours, mentally and physically.'

I'm too tired to argue, too tired to care.

He lays into me eventually for leaving the dishes in the sink. Feeling guilty about the housework going to pot, I spend a couple of nights after work washing, hovering, cleaning and cooking. Then the following day, I flake at work.

Bill decides to help out.

'Don't bother about the shopping this week. I'll do it.'

His shopping consists of buying a couple of tins of meat and veg before stopping off for a pint at the pub. The housekeeping is drunk along with the bills money. I begin to feel as if I'm slowly killing myself doing everything that needs to be done, yet I can't trust him long enough to share the jobs, including shopping for food.

We are taking part in a survey on relationships. I didn't think he would. But then he's completing the questionnaire, sealing it in a large brown envelope ready to post before leaving for work. Unable to resist, I take a peek at his answers, wondering why he's being so shy about sharing them with me. Reading them is a revelation!

He freely admits he can find nothing good in our marriage, and that we constantly bicker. I'm not surprised to read he resents any control over his money and the way it's spent. Our sexual incompatibility I also found very honest, remarkably so, given this is for a stranger. But I'm surprised to see that he fancies group orgies and would like to see me doing it with someone else. I don't know why, but this upsets me. He's being completely open and free with his thoughts. He's rated our happiness as zero, and even gone on to state that, given his chances, he would never marry again.

The truth hurts.

At work, I'm still there three hours after everyone else has gone home. It's physically and emotionally draining. My concentration wavers. And balance the books ... I can't!

'Pull yourself together, for heaven's sake!' the boss tells me almost daily.

1 April 1978

I can't do a thing right. Everyone seems to have complaints. Then around midday life suddenly gets hectic and I find myself in one hell of a mess. Customers are clamouring for attention. Clients hover, waiting to pay bills. The phone refuses to stop ringing even for a moment, and my head still hurts where Bill has struck me the previous night. By dinner, my mind has blown into a zillion little pieces.

I'm tired when I reach home. Bill does nothing to help. He goes out to play with Hot Ayr, leaving me crying upstairs in a pigsty of a house. I just feel so low, so uncared for, so unloved.

12 April 1978

I discover a letter in the back of a drawer replying to an advert of a flat.

'But Jan, you can see our marriage is a farce. We're just pretending, playing at being in love.'

For the first time in all these years we sit and talk like equals … well, almost … rationalising about our crumbling relationship … crumbling? Who am I trying to kid! There was never anything there to crumble in the first place. But hey, we're communicating, actually talking, sharing feelings and … we decide to do the decent thing … to split.

Bill freely confesses he's known I'm at breaking point. While he's not prepared to admit he put me there, he has been preparing to make a run for it, to simply disappear without trace. Now, it seems a relief somehow that I've found the flat he was applying for, because it's better we separate rather than for me to divorce him.

Have I missed something?

He's afraid of the legal hassle. He's scared of .... I don't know. But there's something ... something that's nagging at me. Something I've missed that isn't coming through.

13 – 28 February 1978

I plod around, telling everyone we're separating, that I'm going to Birmingham to be with my parents ... but it doesn't seem real somehow.

I visit the bank, the doctor, the Council, a solicitor, Social Security, numerous other official sources to clarify my position. They all say the same ...

'But Mrs D ..., you are the one who is leaving. You are technically deserting your husband, your marriage. As such, you will be entitled to nothing ... no help whatever from the State. Far better for you to stay home where you belong.'

I know where I stand, at least. It's going to be a long uphill climb.

Evenings are spent calmly making lists, dividing up furniture and household goods ... *how bizarre is that!* At work, I am being sick, having dizzy spells, shaking uncontrollably. Pills don't help any more. Ironically, Bill is the best I've ever seen him. He makes dinner for me ... almost a first! He makes certain I'm comfortable before leaving to play at a gig. Suddenly he's kindness itself now I'm leaving.

Our last night together ... and he takes me out.

'To celebrate,' he says, 'to celebrate our freedom, our liberation.'

The war between us is done.

28 April 1978
Laura and Ralph arrive. They are to drive me to Mum and Dad where I hope to stay until I've straightened myself out. It's going to take time.

'A separation will do you both the power of good,' Mum says, not knowing, not understanding the way my marriage has been, unable to see the scars that mark my body.

'It will give you both time to think things over, to see things in a new light,' muses Dad.

They both harbour this idea that it's only a temporary measure, some kind of holiday, they're not really listening to the truth.

29 April 1978

The day begins in a glorious haze of sunshine. It's hot and humid. I decide on impulse to wear my new summer outfit, bought with the final week's wages from work. Bill accused me of being frivolous.

'Why don't you put your mind to paying off some of these fines and loans? You've complained often enough about them in the past.'

'But they're not mine to pay,' I'd countered.

'We're still man and wife,' he'd been quick to point out. 'What's yours is mine, what's mine is yours.'

The words were right, but somehow the meaning was wrong. Besides, maybe that was what I was missing … that as long as we didn't divorce, I was still liable as his wife for his debt?

Everyday thoughts flash through my mind. I put the kettle on, make tea, tiptoe upstairs to the stirring sleepers. I trip over my suitcase and guitar on the landing, displaced belongings with nowhere to go. It brings the whole sorry business of my life back, putting it in focus. My hands shake uncontrollably as I hand cups to Laura and Ralph.

Today is the day when finally I am leaving my marriage. I left in spirit, now we've to go back to collect my things.

The date has had a red ring around it for some time. Now it's arrived I can hardly believe it's happening. I feel strangely empty as I check the list I'm taking with me. I expect to feel something, maybe even to cry a little. But now I look around the house, the place I had once thought of as home, and I feel like a stranger. I just want to get on and do it … and move on.

There are things which I can't take suddenly … despite our agreement. He's changed his mind. It was always the nature of the beast. He smashes a coffee table hand carved for me some years ago, a particular favourite. He's stamping his control … for the last time. In the end, I sit in the white van Ralph has organised for the occasion, watching things come through the front door one at a time being loaded. And when we're ready for the off, he's sitting on the kerb, his arm around the redhead from down the road.

I wonder …

He doesn't say goodbye. But it doesn't matter. Nothing matters any more except getting away to a new town and strangers who don't know.

May 1978

Mum and Dad are bitter, angry. They can't understand or accept. They're not listening to what I'm telling them. It's hard … admitting the truth after all these years. But then, I can't really tell them at all. How can I? Where are the words to encompass all that pain? And what do they want me to do anyway … they are saying about going back … but that means getting hurt … ultimately, for Bill … *to kill me*? Is that what it will take to truly see the way it is?

In moving me out, Ralph found plugs mis-wired. The gas tap was left on one time when I was so depressed, sitting by the empty grate because we didn't have enough to buy fuel. *Was he capable?* Yes, I think is the answer. *So what is so difficult to understand? Can't they see the marriage is a sham? Can't they see through the façade?* I can't show them my scars. A step too far. I just need them to believe me ... like the child abused by the specialist ... the teenager throwing up before school or going to the home of the music teacher of an evening ... I'm still asking that support, protection, guidance, love. *Can they ever love me ... just the way I am? Is that really too much to ask?*

Alone in my bed at night I cry for the past. Stupid, I know ... what is the past except pain and betrayal? I cry, as if bereaved, for all the broken promises and lies, for all the things I'd hoped would happen but never did. I cry for the child that should have been mine. I cry great pools of tears because I feel so empty, so insecure and so desperately unloved.

I mourn the loss of my husband ... a husband in name only. I'm married but I've never had a husband the way other wives have. I mourn the stability of marriage and a man who would respect and nurture and protect and care for and love. I pine for a place of my own, someone to share the rest of my life. I can't let go. It's so hard suddenly to be alone with all this pain, to cut free from what has been. I count the days since my leaving.

And then I wonder ... *should I go back?*

* * * *

Everything is such an almighty hassle. I have to fight for the smallest thing. I have no money. I queue for what seems like hours at the Unemployment Office, only to be given a sheaf of forms. Shakily my hand hovers over blank boxes, my foggy mind trying to find answers. Then I take my place at the back of another queue.

'But you haven't filled sections D, E, F, H, or J,' states the lady behind the counter.

'I can't,' says I simply.

'Oh come, they're simple enough.'

I feel a fool with everyone listening.

'Now then, which category do you come under … single, married, divorced, widowed?'

She wants to file me, slot me into a place in her card index, a number instead of a name.

'Actually, I'm still officially married, but separated from my husband at this time,' I tried to make it as simple for her as possible.

'I see,' she replies icily, her glare frosty.

I watched her scribble notes in the margin of my form.

'He left you, I take it?'

'No, the other way around. I left him.'

Why suddenly do I feel ashamed at leaving a loveless marriage?

'Now,' she said, leaving that section and moving swiftly on to the next. 'How many children?'

'None,' I'm looking down at the floor.

'Well, have you a doctor's certificate then, with a reason you can't work?

She was getting desperate. She obviously disliked being unable to categorise me, to file me away, to shut the drawer on my life, preparing to send me on.

'No,' I whisper. 'I haven't been to the doctor's yet.'

She tells me to report back in a couple of days and marks me down as a large ominous question mark. I creep quietly away to cry.

*   *   *   *

Evening, and I sit in the doctor's waiting room, waves of self-pity washing over me. My mind keeps working round and round in circles, gnawing at the problem of how to breathe fresh life into a dead marriage. If I take over all the money … if I pay the bills … if I can instill into myself a cool, level head, blanket out the emotion … but deep down it isn't me who needs to change.

I move to a chair at the side of the doctor's desk. I'm shaking from head to foot, unable to keep still, absentmindedly lifting the gold band on and off my finger, my mind picking the petals on the eternal flower ... *'will I go?'* ... *'will I stay?'*

'Now, what can I do for you, young lady?'

He's my father's doctor. I don't know what to say.

'I've just left my husband. I was on anti-depressants ... can you give me something to stop me hurting inside?'

Words spill into the space between, muddled, confused. It wasn't what I had been going to say at all. I'd had it all planned. Now I've made a mess of even this small task.

'Come, come. Everyone has their ups and downs. Go home like a good wife ... kiss and make up.'

He's not understanding ... I try again.

'But he hits me. It took me a great deal to leave, and now I've taken this step I can't go back ... not really. Please, all I need are some pills to tide me over, and a form for the Unemployment.'

I'm crying, pools gathering, an ocean of hurt running free. He motions me to the changing room, examines me on the couch. I breathe in, breathe out. He taps my chest several times, takes my pulse.

'You appear fit enough to me,' finally he pronounces his verdict. 'Can't find anything wrong at all.'

I run out through the door, through the waiting room beyond, past the people waiting to be seen, out to Dad waiting patiently in the car. His comforting arm moves around my shoulder, and a fresh flood of tears begins again.

'He told me to go back, to go home ...'

Dad didn't wait to hear more. He took the surgery by storm, tearing a strip of an astonished receptionist, blasting his way through to see the doctor.

We return home in silence. I run up to my room. Downstairs I hear Mum and Dad having a heated argument. Tempers are flaring. Voices are raised. I wish I hadn't come.

Dad looks like he's aged ten years. I've become something nasty to be swept under the carpet. I feel ashamed ... I've disgraced the family name.

The doctor gives me a certificate eventually, renewing it every seven days for the next month. The same word was on each certificate ... anxiety. Such a trite meaningless word for such a major event in my life. I take it to the lady at the Unemployment. She looks, looks again ... and accepts it coolly. She files it away with the question mark. But still I have no money.

* * * *

The Social Security interviews me in a private office.

'... by law, whether a couple be separated mutually or otherwise, a man must maintain his wife by weekly payments of £13.05,' a Liable Relatives Officer quotes at me … and smiles.

Well, it sounds simple. £13.05 isn't that much. But it's something? But like any other payment that ever was, with Bill it would be in arrears. So what happens then? They call it 'Maintenance', but adds as an afterthought:

'It's a pity there's no children. A child would make all the difference.'

'A difference to whom? I ask no-one in particular.

* * * *

One week after leaving home, I travel back with Ralph and my younger sister's boyfriend Tony. Pulling up outside the house in a van, we prepare to put my half of the furniture on board. I have mixed feelings. Seeing Bill again makes me feel sick. Timidly I knock at the door of what was once my home.

'Come in, everything's ready.' He greets me like a stranger.

His face is set and hard, his eyes stare right through me, gouging, digging, hurting, crawling around my mind. The moment I see him I know that whatever we had between us is gone. This is a drawing of the line.

He sits on the bottom stair while Ralph and Tony traipse backwards and forwards with furniture. He raises no objections, making only one comment the entire time we're there:

'You know, I'm actually enjoying this!'

It seems a bizarre thing to say ... especially given my own feelings are in complete turmoil. I ease past him to stand for the last time in the room that was our bedroom. It seems fitting somehow that it should begin and end here. I avert my eyes from the bed to gaze bleakly out the window. A group of neighbourhood vultures have gathered and I turn away. On a chair is a pile of photograph albums. The top one is open at our wedding. But then every single picture of Bill has been removed. The other pages have been dealt with likewise. It's as if he's blanking himself, taking him away from my past, my life.

Empty of emotion I head for the front door. I turn for the last time and catch Bill's eye. There are no regrets, no tears, no embrace. Why would there be? We smile and wave ...

I whisper goodbye.

Reflections

making sense of a fragile world

So why can't someone leave a loveless marriage, especially one in which they are getting hurt and pain has become an intrinsic part of everyday life?

I have been asked the question many times. Too many people have said they would have left given the same set of circumstances. They ask if I somehow enjoyed the pain, if I am addicted to violence.

No-one enjoys pain to that extent. Even in this book I have withheld so much of the treatment metered out in the name of 'love', in a marriage in which I should never have been a part. In the end, pain became torture. And when someone gets a kick out of seeing someone hurt, inflicting more and more pain in order to increase the hype, then you have to find all kinds of ways to hide the hurt that is happening, avoid the screams, and live the nightmare in silence. That way, you mess with their fantasy ... and they move on to find someone else to torture, needing to hear the screams because it is from that they get their hard-on.

You have to be there to understand. You need to have shared the experience of abuse and all that means to truly appreciate, despite the pain, how hard leaving really is, and why so many return.

One way of understanding is by looking at it in an ABC format …

- **A**ntecedents
- **B**ehaviour
- **C**onsequences

Antecedents are about looking at what came *before* entering the relationship. What was going on in life *before* this episode … however long that episode may be.

I still find it hard, over thirty years on, to accept that my parents may somehow have failed me. *Why*? Because they were my parents. As a small child, you grow up idolising them, putting them on a pedestal where they can do no wrong. Naively perhaps, they believed they were protecting me by keeping me ignorant of the ways of the outside world.

And yet …

My questions were never answered. I never learned to say 'No'. No was not an acceptable form of behaviour … at any age, even after I left home. They didn't teach me to protect myself. They held me apart, keeping me ignorant particularly about my own body. We didn't even acknowledge my disability never mind talk about it, or explain why I was wearing these heavy clompy boots, while all the girls around me wore delicate summer strappy sandals. I was never going to work, never drive a car, never have a normal life. But then, in later life, they denied I'd worn callipers at all. *Shock horror*! And again, as in childhood, I was caught between reality and illusion.

In my early years a chair was never a chair … it was a cave. A sheet on the line was never just that … it was a tent. A cardboard box … a pirate ship. Yes, they were games … childhood games. And yet it was so much more … because suddenly these innate objects took on a whole different persona. *What chair? What sheet? What box?*

What callipers?

My trips to the hospital I found years and years later had been described to my two sisters as 'special'. It caused jealousy with them. They wanted to know why I had been taken on special treats … which meant I was treated different to them, because they had been made to stay at home with a Sitter. When I returned, I was silent, as if withholding secrets. And if I did say anything it was about eating cake in a café, riding on the donkeys at Kennards.

They never knew I'd been to hospital. They can't remember me in callipers because they are so much younger. They only know what they were told, and that wasn't anything to do with the reality of the situation. Misinformation can lead to erroneous beliefs.

And no, this isn't a blame game. It is simply about understanding and answering the question '*Why?*'

I was controlled in a very real way in my growing years. But then that was part of the culture in which we lived. In the 1950s youngsters didn't question their parents. They did as they were told, or risked punishment. There was no Children's Act, and no

243

Human Rights. We lived by the adage '*children should be seen and not heard*'.

I was already conditioned.

I was a good girl, well used to obeying the rules.

That could only make it easier for someone to control me, and maintain that control without fear of me either telling the secret, or breaking free … and taking that control to a whole new level …

Abuse!

And so we come to the 'B' of the ABC formula … Behaviour … which is about what is happening at the time, and why we respond the way we do.

I married my abuser.

Why?

It sounds bizarre … and yes, I can appreciate why people might like to believe I somehow craved attention and pain. But consider what I have just said about my growing years. I was raped when I was 16 years old. At the same time, and I still find this incredibly difficult to get an angle on; I was being sexually abused by a music teacher both at school and his home. They were extraordinary circumstances. Two completely different kinds of abuse running parallel … one very violent and abusive … the other 'specialness' abuse, using the fact I was a victim of bullies, offering a safe haven and abusing that trust. In other words, identifying a need and fulfilling that need … but at a price.

First of all, you need to understand the girl I was then was so much younger than her sixteen years ... not least because of her upbringing. She didn't know the facts of life. She didn't know about periods. She didn't know about her body. She wasn't stupid, but nothing was as it seemed. Brought up on 30s, 40s, 50s music she had no conception of current trends. Because of a lack of money, her clothes came secondhand as and when she could acquire them.

Having a boyfriend made her the same as other girls for the first time in her life. But then she was led down a path leading into an adult world for which she was totally unprepared. She'd always been told sex was dirty, sex was somehow nasty and shouldn't be entered into. I have only to remember the times I was found at the bottom of the garden with Charlie ... the inference being we were doing something very wrong and immoral ... to know that was true. Innocent childhood games, that's all they were. Given what was happening at the hospital, a psychologist later pointed out to me it was a way of working out what was happening through play, as children do. It was a perfectly normal response. But the outcome was that when sex *was* dirty and painful and everything I had been led to believe to be true ... no surprise then ... that was the way it was! Get used to it. You're now entering the realms of the adult world ... the world outside the safe haven of home ... the castle where nothing is as it seems ... and all the stories you've ever heard of the world outside is bad and evil and you'll get hurt big time if you wander from the path your parents set you on.

I was also brought up to believe that the person you do it with is the person you marry. By the time I ended up standing beside my rapist at the altar in front of my minister-father, I knew. I didn't have on rose-coloured spectacles. I'd been a battered girlfriend for five years. This was all I was worth. No-one else would have me. This was my one and only chance at marriage ... or so I believed. At least he accepted me for what I was. Besides, when the prince and princess marry in fairy stories there's always a happy ever after. And I was still naïve enough to believe that to be true!

And so I married my abuser.

The consequences of such actions means I came out of one abusive experience only to fall into another. That is by no means different to anyone else who has been abused. The longer you remain in an abusive environment, the more set you are in his ways ... and the more likely to be targeted by another abuser.

It means you have adopted their mindset.

The reasons I stayed in abuse for so long is the shame, the fact that I had no-one to turn to, nowhere to seek help. I believed it was only happening to me. I had never heard of the concept of abuse. I left two years prior to my eventual leaving, but went back to endure more because there was this idea I couldn't stay with my parents. *But if I didn't, where was I going to go?* Other people have since told me that they could have returned to their parents at any point in their life when things were going wrong, and their parents would stand by them. That was their true home. But when we left home, it was forever. My belongings were not kept for me, but handed to the next one down and then got rid of. I don't know if it was because my father was a minister, because we moved around a great deal, or because they had their own mindset of what should happen within a family, and that once you left home there was no going back.

Abuse happens. It's a fact of life. It's still not talked about even today because of the shame, the stigma ... because of fear of retribution, threats imposed on the victim ... and more than anything else, because of the mindset imposed on the victim through control, often so effective it prevents them ever sharing, ever seeking help.

This mindset has a name recognised in America but still not in the UK. The name of the mindset is '*The Battered Women's Syndrome*'. It is the same mindset used when a child is abused.

There are four ways in which abuse can happen:

- Physically
- Mentally
- Emotionally
- Sexually

Abuse happens across the social spectrum. Anyone can become a victim in whatever form that might take ... at any age ... for however long. Males and females alike become victims, from whatever race, creed, religion and colour.

The Battered Women's Syndrome identifies a pattern of behaviour that a victim will display ... whoever their abuser may be.

Battered Women's Syndrome

To understand battered woman's syndrome, it's important to understand how someone becomes a 'battered woman'. It is also important to understand why battered women stay in abusive relationships.

For understanding to take place, there needs to be compassion, empathy, support ... and even if you don't understand and it's a different world to the one you come from, you have to learn to listen with your heart. More than anything else, leaving abuse means you need a friend, someone you can rely on, who will be there for you, and who will help and enable you to take back control of your life.

There are four characteristics of the syndrome:

- *The woman believes that the violence was her fault.*
- *The woman has an inability to place the responsibility for the violence elsewhere.*
- *The woman fears for her life and/or her children's lives.*
- *The woman has an irrational belief that the abuser is omnipresent and omniscient.*

The Battered Women's Syndrome is considered to be a form of Post-Traumatic Stress - a severe anxiety disorder that develops after exposure to an event resulting in psychological trauma, overwhelming the individual's ability to cope. In psychological terms, it means a woman will -

- *have flashbacks and nightmares,*
- *there will be triggers, everyday things, which will make her feel she is living in her past, re-experiencing the pain,*
- *she will become phobic*
- *suffer extreme anxiety*
- *panic attacks*
- *have difficulty falling or staying asleep,*
- *feel angry without reason, but be unable to do anything about it,*
- *be open to self-harm as a way of either wanting to cut out the bad she perceives is in her, or else showing people how bad she hurts,*
- *be open to anorexia or bulimia as a way of taking control of something in her life when everything else appears beyond her,*
- *feel completely helpless.*

Again, I would emphasise that anyone, regardless of their gender or age, creed or colour, is open to abuse, and in identifying with the syndrome above.

What is a Cycle of Abuse?

A Cycle of abuse is when abuse occurs in a repeating pattern.

Generational cycles of abuse can be passed down, by example, from parents to children. Episodic abuse occurs in repeating patterns within the home. It may involve spousal abuse, child abuse, or even elder abuse.

A son, who is repeatedly either verbally or physically abused by his father, can end up treating his own children in the same way ... because it is his Norm. He needs to work through his experiences, to talk and share and understand them to know he won't do the same for the future. When a daughter hears her mother frequently belittled, criticised by her father, she can so easily adopt that learned behaviour, to the extent she loses respect for her mother completely. Similarly, a child who witnesses his parents engaging in abusive behaviour can unwittingly subject his or her spouse to the same abusive patterns.

That isn't to say that people who have experienced childhood abuse go on to become abusers. It can be that childhood experiences means we become abhorrent of all things abusive and violent, keeping a distance from anyone displaying these tendencies. But our early years are our formative years. They have an impact on the rest of our life and the way we are in relationships.

Even to the extent of the kind of people we choose as our life partners.

It is so important for those leaving a violent marriage and indeed any form of abuse, to understand how they got there in the first place, and learn to change their own pattern of behaviour accordingly to stop abuse happening again.

It is too easy to come out of one abusive relationship and hand control on to another. Taking back control of your life takes courage and strength, one small step at a time. It won't happen until you come to terms with what has happened and given yourself time to get past the effects … or least learn to live with them.

But then, there are two questions needing to be asked -

Do you crave control?

Do you not recognise a controller until it's too late?

In asking myself these questions, I identified that control has been a part of my life since its beginnings. It became my Norm. I am comfortable with it and, without being a victim, I am happy with a controlling influence as part of a *loving* relationship where we are both equals. I gain security and strength knowing ultimately he is the Dominant. I can trust him to make decisions … with *my* welfare and best interests at heart.

In the past, right up to the point of meeting my partner a few years ago, I entered bitter and painful relationships because I had not recognised a controller until it was too late, and I was sucked back into the mindset. I did not realise easily I was under threat ... until I had been hurt again. And recognised the cycle. And got out before it could take hold and took me back into The Battered Woman Syndrome, repeating the same responses as before, adopting the same mindset.

If we are dependants, sometimes it takes a little longer to recognise the signs ... and pull out ... and give ourselves that chance of a better, healthier, happier life.

Stages of Battered Women's Syndrome

There are generally four stages in the Battered Women's Syndrome:

Stage One–Denial
This occurs when the battered woman denies to others, and to herself, that there is a problem. Most battered women will find all kinds of excuses for why their partners have an abusive incident. Battered women will generally believe that the abuse will never happen again ... whereas it will in truth only get worse.

Stage Two–Guilt
This can only occur when a battered woman acknowledges that there is a problem in her relationship. She recognises she has been the victim of abuse and that she will beaten again. There is nothing she can do to stop it coming. It will happen regardless. During this stage, most battered women will take on the blame or responsibility of any beatings they may receive. Battered women will begin to question their own characters and try harder to live up their partners 'expectations.'

Stage Three-Enlightenment
This occurs when a battered woman starts to understand that no one deserves to be beaten. A battered woman comes to see that the beatings she receives from her partner are not justified. She also recognises her partner

has a serious problem. Now she stays with her abuser in an attempt to keep the relationship intact with hopes of future change, somehow believing things will get better, living on Hope.

Stage Four–Responsibility
This occurs when a battered woman recognises that her abuser has a problem that only *he* can fix. Battered women in this stage come to understand that nothing they do or say can help their abusers. Battered women in this stage choose to take steps to leave their abusers and begin to start new lives.

It was Lenore Walker, an American psychologist, who began to identify similar patterns of thinking and behaviour in battered women and gave them the name *The Battered Woman Syndrome*. In the late 1970s she put it forward as a theory to explain domestic violence. It explains the psychological problem in women repeatedly abused by their husbands. The Syndrome entered the legal realm when Lenore Walker gave expert testimony at trials in America of women accused of killing their abuser. However, despite her intention to show that battered women's actions may have been justifiable, that translated in the courtroom as an argument of self-defence.

Eventually, as part of the American *Violence Against Women Act* in 1994, Congress mandated a report on *The Battered Women's Syndrome* role in the courtroom, including its validity and usefulness. The report, *The Validity and Use of Evidence Concerning Battering and Its Effects in Criminal Trials* rejected Walker's syndrome terminology, saying the term "*does not adequately reflect the breadth or nature of the scientific knowledge now available*" (Rothenberg 781). Despite its official rejection by Congress, BWS is still sometimes invoked in American criminal proceedings today.

Leaving abuse, even though it means the more you stay the more you feel the pain; isn't easy. It takes courage. It needs to be done in simple stages. And it becomes a learning process for all concerned. It is impossible to leave with the intention of adopting immediately a new way of life outside and within, drawing a line under what has happened, and move on.

It is common for battered wives to return home.

They mourn the loss of home. It was their home, a home they built up with their partner/husband. They are a living part of it, and it isn't fair that they should have to start again … when what happened wasn't their fault. But too often, it is the victim who leaves, hoping to find a new life.

Many will say '*better the devil you know*', which refers to their absolute mistrust of men. And they will stay because of a fear of going and being alone and starting again and having other people know. It is too easy to get trapped between fears … a fear of staying … a fear of leaving. It can become a no-win situation.

There is also the fear of being attacked by your abuser outside the home, not knowing where he is at any given time, being stalked, having your life disrupted again and again. Yes, there are court orders. But at the end of the day they are just paper. No-one is actually there to enforce the law when you need it most.

And so women go back rather than remain at risk ... or their children being hurt or snatched, believing somehow in the stability of family and keeping them together.

People go back into abuse because the world outside isn't understanding or sympathetic or simply aren't listening to what it is you're saying. I was classed as a *'deserting wife'*. That too is common. You can talk about violence and abuse all you like. But to many lucky enough to live outside that cycle, it's another world. You're living on a different planet. You speak another language. And basically, people don't want it to impinge on their lifestyle or to get involved. Why should they? There is always the chance it might be contagious, they might somehow become alienated, and 'catch' what you have, and themselves be open to abuse. At least, that's what they tell me. It was the way I was treated on leaving.

The family has an essential role. If you leave to stay with parents, what is going on in their lives? How much are they going to listen? How much can you share? Even though they don't understand, will they be there for you? They should be. That's what parents are for. But often, for whatever reason, they let us down and add to the betrayal, and fail us, leaving us on a cliff edge.

For me, it was a tied house that my parents lived in. Maybe there was the fear of Dad losing his job somehow if I stayed, of bringing the family into disrepute ... at least that's how I felt at the time ... a skeleton in the closet. He was a minister. I suddenly appeared. Their response was to say I had been working abroad, and suddenly come home ... I was staying a while until I was settled. I found that hard to swallow. But then, if you become dependent on your parents again ... what can you do but continue to live the lie?

For people coming out of abuse it can feel like being a cardboard cut-out ... living on automatic pilot, unable to feel or show emotion. It's just as if you're a ghost and everything is going on around you, and you're not really a part of it, you're in a bubble, and nothing can touch you any more. You can cross the road in front of a bus or lorry and not get run over. You can jump from a very high building and float down safe. It's just the way it feels. It's part of the trauma. Your mind can't handle it. And so it shuts down, and you function just the way you've always functioned as a human being ... a human robot ... nothing more. You do the things you have to do each day, like brushing your teeth, having a shower, washing your hair, putting on clothes, etc, but you can't do any more.

Endings & Beginnings

Life can be a long lesson in humility

May 1978

I left my past life at the end of last month. Now I have at least some of my own things around me and can sleep in my own bed. I thought somehow this would make everything better. I can move on. Period. But it's hard, so different from my normal routine. And I can't talk about anything that happened to me. They don't understand. They're not even listening … just continuing on with their own lives, putting up with the inconvenience I've become. At least that's how it feels to me right now.

I miss my cheery milkman, miss being in my own home with a back door and a garden. I keep catching myself thinking of what I'd normally be doing. But then at the same time I'd be on edge. As the day wears on, I'd be waiting for the scrape of the key in the door, wondering what kind of mood he'd be in, hoping it would be different, ready with a smile, knowing what would come.

Too many memories crowd my mind. At times I feel like screaming to make the world understand. Mum and Dad are like sticking plasters, hiding wounds which continue to fester and hurt.

It's strange how I can blank out the bad times. Like having tunnel vision, suddenly nothing is quite so bad. *If I go back ... things will be different?* I feel so isolated, so alone, rejected, abandoned, betrayed. It's like being the black sheep of the family and the guilt lies heavy on my shoulders. I'm constantly hearing apologies and excuses made on my behalf. I've brought shame on my family.

Mum and Dad start to draw a veil over what has been. I haven't talked or shared, they don't know, they can't even imagine what my life was like, but suddenly, I'm introduced into their social circle as their single daughter who has been working abroad. I hide my gold band in company, but wear it in private, as if keeping hold of my true identity. I don't want that particular identity, but then I don't want either the one my parents are hoisting on me. I learn to make do with threesomes, always being one of a crowd, never being alone for long. Everyone is falling over themselves, and it is stifling, so much so that I take to walking, cycling, playing tennis, taking my frustrations out on a ball. It becomes routine to tire myself out so that at night I am too tired to think.

My doctor congratulated me before I left home:

'This is the break you needed ... well done! All it needs is time ... you need to give it time ... and you will become a new woman.'

He knew how hard it had been to leave, in the end. His words felt good, at the time. Now time is something I have in abundance. I had naively expected everything to come right as soon as I left Bill, for my health to return, my shaking to stop, and the man of my dreams to step into my life with that happy-ever-after-ending, and everything to come right. It's all taking so long.

I walk along a busy Birmingham street on a sunny Saturday afternoon. It hurts to see a couple holding hands, love and happiness shining on their faces. *Will I ever feel that way?* It shows me not only what I'm missing now, but what I've missed in my lifetime. I don't know what it feels like to be loved in that way! An ache starts deep in the pit of my stomach as a bouncing baby bumps past in a pram. And I remember Bill's words as we decide to split: '*You know, I wouldn't let you go if we had a child. You'd be mine for all time then*'. I have to be grateful for that, at least … but it hurts … how desperately it hurts.

Relatives are writing, sending condolences, wishing me well. What did they know? But then, I feel as if I'm on trial. Any friends I had in Birmingham drop me like a hot potato. I've become a threat, an outcast, betrayed by my own kind. *Why?* … because I'm single and marrieds feel threatened. They don't want me around.

Over weeks that follow I fall into a decline, living in a state of suspended animation, walking in a dream. Figures float past me in a mist. I refuse to see beyond my depression. I withdraw totally from the world. My tablets become my lifeline. They stop me hurting, switch off my mind. I get up at midday and walk aimlessly around. I play the piano, sing songs of women lamenting loved ones gone to war. Days drift idly by.

June 1978

Mum and Dad take me on holiday to Portsmouth. Ralph and Laura come too. It's good to get away. Slowly I feel myself come alive again. There are new interests to occupy my time. And in returning to Birmingham, I start looking for a job. My term of mourning for the death of my marriage is over.

I visit a solicitor to start divorce proceedings. It is on his advice I make a list from my diaries of past events. This is the first time I have allowed myself to dwell on them since leaving and they make heavy reading. Friends told me to just up and go. I'd no children to keep me there ... so why stay? I didn't understand it myself. But perhaps it was that I had lived on hope for so long it was difficult to give it up, to admit defeat and myself and my marriage a failure?

Unexpectedly I have a new gleam in my eye. Mum notices first. She's watching me eyeing all the eligible bachelors. There's a young man in the park who sits next to me after a particularly gruelling game of tennis.

'Lovely day,' I begin casually.

'Yes, and you look like you were having a good game on the courts.'

He'd noticed! He'd noticed ... *me*!! I blush furiously, trying to cover my confusion.

'Do you play?'

'Oh, I used to. Now I always seem so busy.'

He begins to tell me about his love for photography. Then, after about half an hour, just as we're getting settled, he looks at his watch. I wonder for one fleeting moment if he's about to ask to see me again … arrange a date … time … place …

'Heavens! My wife will be getting worried.'

I crash down to earth with a bump.

'Nice talking to you. Really must go. She's expecting our third child …'

My dream scatters in a zillion pieces.

'You don't want to fall for the first man who shows you some attention,' Mum warns after.

'You'll only come to grief, end up making a complete fool of yourself again.'

But I feel trapped. I resent her remarks. She doesn't know … how can she? Now I've returned home it's like teenage years, I have to be in by nine, always saying where it is I'm going, who I'm going with. And it's not as if I know anyone who can lead me stray.

I buy a *Singles* magazine and mull over their adverts in my room. There are pages and pages of them … lost souls … all seeking someone to love. *I'm not alone*! Mum sighs heavily, tut-tutting in that way she has when she disapproves. Three in particular take my fancy and I wonder if I dare answer. I'm still unsure of myself, so insecure, so lonely. I've never had the chance for love … not true love … perhaps this is the gateway through.

It's my birthday coming up. Why not?

Box 2241 is open, honest, direct:

'Leftwing folksinger, 31, 5'5", seeks female singing partner with view to relationship. Voice unimportant, commitment vital. Car and house.'

I write back, trying to inject a light-heartedness I don't feel. I don't want to sound inhibited or introspective. If we meet, I'm going to be someone different … alive, outgoing, positive, direct.

'Dear Advertiser,

A leftwing bachelor – I wonder what you mean by that? My main interest is music. I sing, play guitar and piano, as well as writing my own songs. I enjoy good company and good food, as well as drives in the countryside, although I must admit to not being able to drive myself. By the way, I note you don't say what your interests are. Perhaps you could give me some indication of these?

I am 25 years old next month, and five foot plus high. My hair is curly auburn, my figure curvy. Basically, it could be said I am a 'home-loving' bird, although I do have outside interests. I wonder what your likes and dislikes are?

I should be glad to exchange photos with you if and when you write …'

My family seem to think I'm going to get hurt on the rebound. Maybe they're right. But I can't just sit here, loused up with memories, seeing life pass me by.

1 July 1978
Dad brought the reply to me as I sat sipping my first cup of tea of the day in bed, hovering expectantly to see what it said:

'*Dear Janine,*

Glad to get your letter, which has rather shaken my confidence in my ad. I didn't think I'd need to be more specific in describing myself as a leftwing bachelor! I'd be pleased to discuss this and many other matters, either on the phone, or preferably in person.

Briefly, I am also centrally involved with music. I've been a resident singer in a Folk Club since 1970, and I've gradually developed instrumental abilities over the years. I play guitar and dabble in several other instruments. I've also written a few songs.

Our circle of friends at the Club provides me with plenty of that 'good company' that I, like you, enjoy so much. Good food likewise, leading to dietary problems, but it's difficult to stop doing something as enjoyable as eating.

We organise regular weekend camping sessions in Wales, which give us a chance to do ten mile hikes over the mountains, and provides great entertainment around the camp fire and in the pub.

264

*To that extent, I like the countryside! As for driving,
I enjoy that greatly, thanks in no small part to my
car which is a prized possession. It's a 1973
Porsche, a giant-killer with oodles of character.
In addition to finding these interests in common with
you, I am also very fond of photography on a semi-
professional basis, reading, games and puzzles,
Bridge, Chess, Scrabble, fringe theatre. I am also
home-loving (though I'm in a love-hate relationship
with this one!)*

*If you are able and inclined, I'd much appreciate a
phone call today between half-five and six, then we
can arrange something. I can't find a photo of me to
enclose, but I'm short at 5'5", with ginger hair, and
a beard of small proportions. I'll take you as you
come – what's inside is so much more important!*

All the best, Melvyn T

He sounds warm, genuine … a man I can trust? He
says he will accept me just the way I am. My kind of
man, with many interests and talents. I've already made
up my mind to follow this through, but his final
sentence clinches it. To know that what is inside me
matters so much more than what I look like gives me
the confidence I need.

*   *   *   *

I hear his voice on the phone … *and I know*! I've tried
to contain myself until 6 o'clock not to appear eager.
My fingers have fumbled their way around the dial.

'Hello … hello, is that Melvyn …?'

265

'Yes, who's that?'

His voice sends shivers down my spine.

'Janine. You said to phone between half-five and six, and ...'

I'm waffling, words chasing ahead of my thoughts.

'Hello Janine.'

He sounds cool, quietly confident, yet at the same time warm and friendly. I miss his next few words. I'm too busy dreaming of all the possibilities this encounter might bring. I can't help it. I know it's stupid. How can it happen just like that? I should be giving myself space ... time ... I need to get over what has happened in the past never mind be setting myself up again ... probably for another fall.

And yet ...

'Would you like me to meet you somewhere for a drink and a chat? Or maybe you'd prefer me to pick you up at your house?'

Mmmm ....I opt for the latter, suddenly needing to meet on home ground, or maybe subconsciously is it that I need my parents' approval?

* * * *

As I wait for him to arrive, strange feelings surge through my body. Deep down, I have that longing to be loved. My whole body is crying out for a man ... and to be loved. That's the simple honest truth. I'm pent up,

266

moody, frustrated, too ashamed of my feelings to sit down and analyse exactly what is going on. And yet I shouldn't be this way ... but then, how should I be? And yes, I know ... I know ... *I know* ... I should simply be taking this as meeting up, having a chat, going out, maybe taking it from there, maybe not, no pressure. But when you've come through what I've come through there isn't any right or wrong way to deal with this kind of situation. I know I'm putting something in motion that I might not be able to stop. And what worries me more than anything else is the S word ... *Sex*.

I've always shied away from it and yet that moment is going to come ... and always it's something that has come up and grabbed me right where it hurts. Because of my experiences, sex means rape. I can't get past that. I wouldn't know how to handle an advance. And if he came on strong, hey ... I'd have my hands right up there and simply take the attitude *'okay, get on with it, I'll lie back and think of the Empire, create a shopping list, or something ...'* I don't know how to say 'No'. Such a stupid little word that has *so* much meaning ... and still, it isn't in my vocabulary.

* * * *

The moment his hand reaches through the front door there is something strange and familiar. And yet we've never met. I don't dwell on it then ... and it's years and years later when finally that particular puzzle is put to rest. Because he has the same hand ... the same hands ... as the music teacher who sexually abused me at his home ... fat, short, stubby digits. I can't take my eyes off the hand coming through the door. His heels click sharply together. My head jerks up. But not before I've taken in the Jesus sandals, at odds with the brown gnome-like image dressed in worn trousers and zip up jumper. Then there is the goatee beard and matching red hair, the large spectacles, and the bullfrog eyes holding me firm in his gaze.

I shake his hand formally as it's offered. He thrusts forward … a busy, bustling body bristling with energy, full of self-importance, knowing exactly what he wants.

'I think we ought to sing.'

His words come as he spies the piano in the lounge. Mum is watching from the kitchen, Dad peeking from behind the study door, my sisters giggling on the landing.

'I'll go make coffee.'

I leave him sitting in the front room and shut the door, fleeing to the kitchen for a breather. It's happening too fast. Where was the foreplay, the customary '*getting-to-know-you' routine?* Mum is wearing that '*I told you so'* expression as I load a tray and tentatively head back towards the guest. What I'm wearing is all wrong … but then I'd look strange suddenly walking in dressed different. Besides, in his letter didn't he say he'd simply accept me just the way I am?

Assuming more confidence than I feel, I slip back into the room to hear him playing my twelve-string guitar. He can play … I mean, he can *really* play! When it's my turn I'm fumbling my usual four-finger pluck, aware of watchful eyes. *What's the matter with me?*

I've played in front of people before. *Why feel this inadequate now? Does it really matter that much?*

I cut the performance short and, clutching the body of the instrument for comfort, try to change the subject.

'I like your car.'

The purple Porsche sits solidly outside the window, its sleek lines gleaming under the street lamp.

'It's a 1973 model, a 911S, with a 2.4 litre engine …'

An enthusiast! I'm struggling to keep pace with facts and figures that spill from his mouth, interjecting an odd murmur of approval between sentences, watching the way his face comes alive as he warms to the theme.

His hands rest neatly in his hip pockets. He stands almost to attention, feet planted firm on the floor. I want to reach out, to know how his hand fits in mine, to understand if this is a man who will honestly and truly respect and love me and never let me go.

'Do you know much about cars?'

His question is a challenge. Something in my expression? Our eyes lock. Is there a spark of the same longing in him? For a fleeting moment I think I see it … or then again it could be something mirrored from my own.

'No, I'm sorry. I hardly know anything about cars.'

He sits suddenly. Oh dear, disappointed.

'Look, time's pressing on. Shall I take you to a folk dance or something?'

Is he hastening the end of our meeting? I don't want to share him with others. This might be the only time we're together to talk … to share … to treasure every moment.

'I'd rather go a ride in your car.'

I excuse myself on the pretext of getting a coat and converse with Mum and Dad in whispers at the top of the stairs.

'Doesn't he talk a lot! How's it going, Pet?'

'Oh fine,' I murmur, trying to keep my voice light. 'We're just going for a drive.'

'D'you think you should … I mean, you hardly know the man?'

A look of concern passes between them. Now is not the time to start a heated discussion about letting their daughter make up her own mind.

I clatter down the stairs. Melvyn is already at the front door. Mum and Dad see us off. I make introductions, knowing they're giving him the once over.

'Don't wait up,' I fling casually over my shoulder.

It's an act of defiance given they've been asking every time I go out when I'll be back, '*be in for nine …*', needing to know if I'm meeting anyone, who I'll be with … as if I have any friends anyway. I mark my boundary before putting thoughts of them firmly out my head and set out to enjoy myself.

The evening passes in a dream. We drive for some time in silence. I gaze up into the clouds as we race across Spaghetti Junction, down through the tunnels, up the other side, and away on the open road. I'm making secret wishes with myself, urging anyone watching from on high to watch over this pathetic needy person on the ground, and save her from coming to any harm.

I realise with a start I'm still wearing the gold band around my finger. I'm flicking it up and down, and wonder if he's noticed.

'I suppose you noticed my wedding ring?'

'*Er … no …* no I didn't.'

He looks surprised. His voice is now sharp. Silence suddenly hangs heavy. I feel the need to justify.

'I'm separated. I'm divorcing my husband.'

It sounds formal. But … how to begin? Where are the words to put it all in a nutshell?

'I think I'd better take you to my place. We'll talk there.'

The decision is made. The car travels at speed and I watch clouds scudding across the sky, like fears racing for the horizon. How is this going to go? But then, we're the product of our past. How can I ignore that? And right from the very beginning I don't want any secrets between us.

The car skids to a sudden halt. I'm surprised … shocked even … that he would live in such a run-down area and yet own such an expensive car. I had expected a cottage in the country, a house with a garden and view, anything but this … a corner plot with a house in bad need of repair, a concrete surround. Inside, uncarpeted floors and peeling walls. Only two rooms in the whole place showed any care and attention … a bedroom decorated in gold and brown, and a studio with thousands of pounds of recording equipment, with egg boxes fixed to the walls as a cheap form of sound proofing.

Do these two rooms depict the main two areas of his life? Are these what matter most? If so, the former has me worried.

But then:

'Right … let's start by … well, you'll see. Come here … sit there … put these on, listen and observe.'

I sit confused. He's taken charge. A pair of heavy headphones are hoisted over my ears blocking out sound. He twiddles and twists knobs. I raise a finger as instructed according to whether or not I hear any sound.

'*Mmmm* ….'

He's not impressed. But then:

'Use my guitar and sing me one of your songs.'

Usually I'd do this with my eyes shut. Now I fumble, my fingers wooden, unconnected. He's observing me. And before I've even got through two lines:

'Enough. As I thought. We'll need to work on that some. And your breathing is all wrong.'

He wants me to shout at walls, standing at the back of me, hands on my hips. But I can't do it. I feel stupid. All I want really is to sit and talk and share and to come to know this man.

We end up in the kitchen, and with a couple of mugs, move to sit in the cluttered front room. There's no TV. He doesn't believe in newspapers or commercialism. Home doesn't mean home in the same way as me. He's a bachelor, a freelance Computer Consultant. As such, all he needs is a building to house belongings and sleep in at night. It seems an empty, lonely life. No wonder he's advertising for a relationship.

We talk around the kind of qualities we are looking for in other people. I share a little of my past, testing the waters, watching his response. He's shocked even at the little I tell him. He's a gentleman, someone who walks ahead and opens doors for ladies to pass through, pulling back seats for them to sit down. It's totally beyond his comprehension that someone would treat a lady any other way.

I'm warming to him. He's a ready listener, easy to talk to. But I don't want his sympathy. I don't want him to feel sorry for me. I want him to make life better … to want me, need me, love me … to take me for his own.

And yet, even now, there is the smallest warning bell ringing in my ear. Our evening, our first meeting has passed … like an interview? It's like he's testing me … and I'm falling far short.

It's two in the morning when we drive back, sitting under the street lamp outside my parents, eking out the evening, not wanting it to end. We've still not touched. We talk and share and it feels like a release. I've felt barriers come down. It leaves me with a need to cling on, to cry out my love for him. *Love at first sight*? I never thought about it before. I somehow believed you need to get to know someone, to spend time with them … *but now?*

'I'll pick you up at seven tomorrow.'

'Tonight', I whisper, smiling in the darkness. Curtains are twitching at the upstairs window. I make for the front door. The Porsche pulls away.

2nd July 1978

Still sailing on Cloud 9. Cannot yet get the wonderful evening and Melvyn, the man of my heart, out of my mind. I am so lucky to have found someone like him. I would be prepared to give my all if things keep on as they are. But is that enough, with all he has to offer?

I feel already I have known him a lifetime. He has a passion for people, and doesn't just talk, but is prepared to act for what he believes in. He's not afraid to get involved. It's incredible the number of interests he has: photography, folk music, trains, drama production. None of these he plays around with or takes lightly. He has seen from experience what it is to love and be rejected, to give but receive nothing in return. I feel for him something which I cannot begin to describe. Is it love?

The hours till we meet stretch interminably. I try to fill them, to keep busy, sleeping late, then replaying the evening over and over like a gramophone record. All I can think of is him.

As evening approaches, he arrives as promised, to take me to a folk club. I try not to mind sharing our time with friends. I put on my social face, hide my inhibitions and shyness. He treats me as a friend, one of the crowd, nothing special. But then, his hand touches mine … only for a moment … as he reminds me of our pact to follow his special starvation diet. I sip my single tomato juice and concentrate on following the words of the unfamiliar chorus everyone is singing around me.

3rd July 1978

I wake feeling vibrant and warm and snugly inside. I feel like I've never felt before … and again … *is this Love*? Does it happen just like that? Is it too soon? I know I'm vulnerable, needy. But I hug myself, wishing they were his arms around me. We'd sat under the same street lamp talking until almost 3am. Now I'm finding it hard to get up for my part-time cleaning job. But I need

275

the distraction, to block out time and thought and this evening ... it can't come soon enough.

He arrives punctual as ever, and drives me to his house. But then, something is different. I'm frustrated, knotted, tensed. We sing a little and the strain is right there in my voice. He shows me breathing exercises to relax. His hands tag on my hips and a tremor runs the full length of my spine. I half turn to throw my arms around him, catching myself in time. He moves away ... the moment is past.

Then later, in the silence:

'You want it, don't you?'

I drop my eyes from the intensity of his gaze.

'Come on, stop playing games.'

Blushing furiously now, I'm uncertain without being deliberately coy. I don't know how to handle this situation.

'I don't know what you mean.'

My pulse quickens. I'm afraid of what I feel inside. It's the moment I have dreaded ... *so why do I want it so much?*

For the next ten minutes or so we bandy words back and forth before finally reaching a decision.

'I will if you will.'

'All right then.'

We rise as one. I'm looking at him to lead, and in the hallway, hang back, again uncertain.

'Come on, I won't hurt you.'

Were they Bill's words ... or Melvyn? Past and present are merging. I'm not certain where I am any more. I'm pressing back against the wall. The world is shrinking around me. I need to be a mouse, small and insignificant. No, a butterfly to flutter away. Or a bird ... a tiny insect ... something ... anything ...

He takes my hand and we nudge one another up the stairs, one step at a time. The bedroom is dark, the bed spotlit by a full moon. It's surreal. I feel like I'm acting out a part in a play. In a trance, I remove clothing, place it neat in a pile, playing for time. When finally I am done, I'm like a puppet with no-one working my strings. This is totally outside my experience.

Melvyn is kind, gentle, considerate, everything a man should be to a woman. But it's still difficult, painful, clumsy. We finger, fidget, fumbling through the overtures. The rhythm isn't right. We're falling out of sync. Then, just as we're settling ... the phone rings beside the bed. I'm ready to let it continue ... but he grabs the instrument ... and talking for the longest time.

The spell is broken. I start to rise. But the receiver clatters down and we begin afresh. Slowly ... oh so slowly, the feeling creeps back ... inching its way... pulling us together. And then its gathering me into its folds until it bursts like a spring bulb, its shoots rising after a long hard winter through the ground into the light of a new dawn. It lasts but seconds ... and yet, to me, it is a moment so beautiful. A single sound escapes my lips ... more than a groan ... it's a cry coming from deep down inside. For the first time ever ... I feel fulfilled.

There are no words to say it the way it is. Yet it's as if he understands. *Has he been there too*? I climb over the summit of the mountain. I'm tired, drained of emotion, and yet feel an almost suffocating awareness of ecstasy. I'm crying. As I stare up at the ceiling, I know I have waited years for this moment. It has triggered something that craves more, leaving me wanting to be satisfied further.

'I'm sorry, Jan ... this isn't going to work.'

Eh!

'You're on your own. It was a joint decision we do this and I don't want any comeback. Y'hear? I don't want you to come crying to me if you're pregnant. You can't be that naïve that you didn't know what you were doing.'

What's going on?

'Come on, grab your coat, I'm taking you home.'

In a state of shock I'm being hussled into the car. During the drive he keeps hammering his points home. And I have absolutely no idea what I did that was wrong.

'We can still be friends, can't we?'

I can't bring myself to cut loose completely.

'Yes, of course. Let me know how you're doing every once in a while. Don't think I don't care simply because we're severing our ties.'

He makes it sound like it's a joint decision, like I know what's going on. And pregnant? My God … *No!* Mum and Dad's faces stare back at me, horrified, mortified.

But it occurs to me he's scared … scared of the very thing he's been searching for so long … someone to love … and commitment. The older we are the more baggage we drag behind us.

'You see, I have this kind of mental image of the kind of person I am looking for … and well, somehow you don't fit.'

He's still trying to explain, to rationalise his fears.

'I have to experience this '*wow*' feeling, so I'll know this is the person for me. I'm sorry, I didn't feel that with you. Not at all.'

I obviously don't fit into his scheme of things. And it's hard to let go. There's nothing left to say. We stare at one another under the same street lamp that has shared so many secrets in such a short time. And then, crying inside, I say goodbye.

4 July 1978
My birthday. 25 years old. *Da-dah* ….

I feel dead inside, like something has come and gone and eaten me all up inside. How can life be so cruel?

Have I fallen for Melvyn because he's all the things Bill is not? Maybe it's my mistake … and if so I would do well to learn from it … and move on.

Two more Singles replies arrive in the post. John is a 29 year old professional bachelor. Charles is a 'graduate recluse'. John's letter is facetious, full of puns. He'll at least take my mind off Melvyn … for the moment.

He arrives outside my parent's house in a sparky yellow Lotus Europa. He had to bend his six foot frame just to get in through the doorway where he stood, hovering uncertain in the hall. Shaking of hands, all very civil, with Mum and Dad, and it wasn't lost on me this time as Mum rushed to the window armed with notebook and pen to scribble down his car number … just in case!

Outside, with long leggy strides, he reaches the car. I sink into a fur-lined seat, almost kneeling on the pavement, slipping gradually inside. I try desperately to think of something intelligent to say as I look sideways at the driver.

'Nice car.'

With a set line to his lips, he twitches them into a smile as we roar off down the road. A packet of cigarettes appears in his hand. He offered them to me and I shake my head. Smoke curls upwards. I'm trying hard not to cough. *Ugh … a smoker*! Not a good start. Blurred images filter through from the past. I wince as I remember the pain of the butt stubbed out on my flesh, the way he'd play with fire, hot ash flicking on my left nipple which remains hidden and inverted ever since.

Is this the way my life is going from now on, fleeing an abusive past, and yet at the same time carrying it with me, plagued by images of pain? Will I hop hopefully from one male to another, searching an elusive love that only exists in fairy tales?

We draw to a screaming stop in the car park of a golf clubhouse. He's obviously well known. His arm goes up and down almost in salute as we pass people he recognises. I follow falteringly in his footsteps. Again, I wonder if I'm dressed for the occasion. It looks posh. But then we're side stepping tables laid for dinner, heading for the bar. A high stool … and I'm still scrambling to get comfortable as he orders a pint of bitter and a coke for me. Then he's sitting wrapped in his own thoughts.

Suddenly, and completely without warning, he slams down his glass and is up and off, heading for the outside door. It takes me moments to realise he's gone. It isn't possible to slip elegantly off a stool meant for a six footer … when I'm only five foot tall. My skirt catches on the far side. I'm grappling with it, trying to look as if I'm used to this situation, while my face flushes hot. A man sitting next to me sees my difficulty and reaches down to unhook me. I'm eternally grateful. It would be so much easier to stay with him, but then I'm scurrying off like a frightened rabbit after the one I came in with.

The car roars impatiently. I'm hardly settled before we hit the road, taking a bend fast. We zigzag in and out of lay-bys, and I hardly dare blink in case I miss something. Next minute we're screaming to a halt. I glance sideways … and stiffen.

'How about it then?'

My seat becomes horizontal … from sitting to lying in one easy movement. I never even saw the lever let alone his hand move towards it. But then, he takes one look at my set expression, my frozen body, my trembling hands, then, crashing the gears, takes off at speed. We make one further stop at a small country pub where he leaves me at a table to go chat to his policeman friends, before we're back in the car and heading back.

It's early as we park up outside my parents' house.

'See you around.'

He's quietly lighting a cigarette, acting as if I've completely wasted his time, waiting for me to go. His fingers drum the dashboard. He glances at his watch.

'Sorry if I'm keeping you up!'

I'm angry, disappointed, upset, confused.

'Maybe I'll give you a ring sometime.'

I slam his door … *hard!*

'Needn't bother,' I mutter as the car speeds away.

5th July

'Graduate Recluse' has arranged to spend the day with me, take me for a meal, followed by a show. *Sounds good*! In many ways he's like Melvyn. His voice has that gentle, reassuring quality on the phone, describing himself as 5'3", 31, with beard and moustache. He works with computers. I have high hopes for this meeting.

I open the door to a small nervous individual peering short sightedly ahead. His glasses are pushed up high on his nose, like a couple of thick glass bottoms. At his insistence, we shake hands formally on the doorstep before he steps inside. There's an awkward silence once we're seated in the front room, coffee cups on laps. Mum and Dad together with my sisters have now entered the selection process and we sit together, he and I beside one another on the sofa. A beard effectively hides his face almost totally from view, and I try not to mimic his habit of bending forward to peer at everything and everyone in the room.

As his hands start exploring, roaming my arm, reaching over my body, worming around my back, my neck, playing with my hair, my sisters start giggling. But he doesn't seem to notice, or maybe he doesn't care.

'What would you like to do this afternoon?'

We start talking at the same time and immediately there is laughter.

'Well, I wondered if you'd like to visit Aston Hall?'

He was anxious to please.

'But please, tell me what *you* would like to do. I'll take you for a meal and we can properly get to know one another. I'm sure we're going to be fine.'

His tatty off-white Morris Minor makes a change from the cars I've been driving around in recently. But I'm far from happy as we cruise carefully down the centre of the road, perfectly straddling the centre white line. He hunches over the wheel, seemingly oblivious to the angry hoots of other motorists passing by.

He's a mild man by nature, totally incapable of a cross word. Anger is an alien concept. Maybe that's one reason I'm warming to him. As people crush in front of us at Aston Hall, the Guide leaves us behind. But Charles takes me gently by the arm as if showing me off as his prize.

It's a pleasant day. I'm made to feel like a Queen. Nothing is too much trouble. He just wants to please me and for everything to go well between us. I'm beginning to believe he's the gentlest, kindest, most loving man imaginable.

Later in the cinema he whispers:

'You're the one for me.'

'But we've only just met.'

Now it's my turn to be cautious. Maybe I'm learning.

'I know. But I feel it … right here.'

His hands reach for mine and place them over his heart. I'm touched. He doesn't need to explain. I feel the same way … about Melvyn. I've placed him on a pedestal just as this man is doing with me. Suddenly, I realise what it feels like. That's what was wrong, what Melvyn resented in our relationship. But then again, for moments I am tempted. Even if I don't feel for Charles in quite the same way as he does me, maybe the feelings might grow through the years?

Memories of Melvyn hold me back.

Later we sit on the sofa at my parents' home watching a late night film. Time ticks on until the white dot is all that's left on the screen. His arms are wound around me, an octopus, he's holding me close every which way and I can't break free. He talks about a cottage in the country … a baby Grand … shopping delivered … everything I could possibly need or wish for … being looked after, protected, loved … I'd never have to leave the cottage … not for anything … ever.

A bird in a gilded cage!

Painting a picture of possibilities, of the way our life would be, he's aroused. I can feel the bulge in his trousers. He wants me so bad. Now it's time to say goodbye and he's reluctant to leave.

'I'll call you later in the week, but promise me, you will think seriously about what I have said, what it is I am offering you, my Lady? A white wedding … a little church … and then you are mine … mine always and forever and …'

'I promise I'll think about it, Charles.'

It isn't a lie. I do have a lot of hard thinking to do over the next few days. But then, at the front door, he turns. I feel like a painting on display. I'm about to speak, but he places a finger to my lips.

'Let me remember you as you are, spotlit by the moon.'

A romantic. I watch him pull on his driving gloves, very precisely, pressing each finger firm. Then, with a last lingering look, he leaves … and I know he is gone from my life … forever.

9 July 1978
'Hello Melvyn, it's Janine.'

My voice is shaking.

'Hello.'

He's surprised. I'm surprised I'm even considering going down this route. But then, given the alternatives I've just tried, he's back on the menu … despite him believing otherwise.

'How are things going?'

Okay, so I've caught his interest. I try keeping any emotion out of my voice as I make my next few moves.

'Well, I've lost half a stone since we met.'

'Really?'

Now he's suitably impressed. But there's an awkward silence. I'm treading carefully. I don't want to frighten him off. I need to bait the trap to catch him unawares.

'Melvyn …? Could you, I mean, would you … *erm* … consider taking me with you to the folk club again this evening?'

I'm holding my breath. I hardly dare move. The atmosphere is electric. He can't know how much it has taken me to make this phone call.

'Look, we agreed it was over. I'll give you instructions how to get there. But that's all.'

Not quite what I hoped for … but it was a start. He starts offering me street names, bus times. I muddle him with my poor knowledge of Birmingham. It takes fifteen minutes … but then he sighs:

'I suppose you think I'm a pig as I've got a car and could so easily take you myself?'

'Yes, I do,' I replied simply and honestly, unusually forthright.

The battle is won.

*   *   *   *

The purple Porsche pulls up outside the house. I stand for moments in front of the mirror. This has to be perfect. I have to do it right. And no emotion … I have to leave it behind. Downstairs, Mum opens the door. I fidget nervously with my skirt, then calmly collect my coat from the rail.

'Coming?'

I throw the word over my shoulder as if I don't really care one way or the other. I've climbed into a new role and I'm trying it out, ironing out the creases. I wait by the car. He catches up and I carefully keep my distance. Through the whole drive, I keep the conversation light and inconsequential, my mind empty of thought.

Once at the Club I make for someone I met last time, and stand talking, trying in some small way to assert independence. And yet, all the while, my eyes rarely leave the bustling body, busily setting up tapes and mikes to record singing. As I sit next to him I focus on the guest of the evening, heartily joining in each chorus. I'm beginning to feel a part of it, soaking up the atmosphere, creating an identity, making it as if this is the family I belong to now.

The best part of all comes when we're driving home. I talk to him about the two men I've gone out with. Now he's genuinely surprised ... and pleased ... and something more ... *almost jealous*?

He applauds my determination to carry on, hopefully seeing me in a new light. We talk some more under the street lamp, and arrange to meet the following evening.

'Purely on the grounds of friendship.'

He's drawing the boundaries, settir
don't care. We passed the first ⊢
meet again!

10 July 1978
Melvyn seems unusually unsure of himself.

'Look Jan, I have something to say, and it's hɑ

I sit on the edge of the sofa, gripping the seat, taking deep breath. I'm not certain what is going on.

'I know I've treated you bad, and I'm sorry, but …'

The 'but' remains hanging between us a long long time before he speaks again. Meanwhile I'm trying to guess what he's going to tell me. Inwardly I'm preparing for the worst. I'm sure this is the finale.

'I've been a fool, Jan. Forgive me. It's been staring me in the face all along. I just couldn't see it. I was blind to my own emotions. Then, when I saw you the other night, I knew. Can we give us another chance?'

I remain absolutely still. I can't move, can't breathe, can't … *I don't dare*. His words float around me. I just want to hear them again.

'Jan … do you hear me? I'm asking for another chance. But I want to make it clear that I must be free to follow other opportunities if they come along.'

I wish he hadn't said those last words … I really really do. But then, even the smallest chance of happiness is

an none. I try to ignore the risk. And then hands
owards me and we're locked in an embrace.

his must be how it feels to be young and in love for
very first time. I just know I'm going to have a hard
e convincing my parents about what is happening.
n the one hand they make it clear that my staying with
them is short lived. And I have nowhere else to go. I
have little money coming in from the DSS, £6 per
week. So no hope there of finding a place of my own.
On the other hand they feel I'm wrong in creating a
new life outside, in going with Melvyn, in starting
another relationship.

Melvyn takes the rest of the month off to finally
make up his mind. I move in with him shortly after. It
seems Mum and Dad have plans to move to a new
ministry in the north next year. Even if I stayed with
them I'd be moving. But then again, we come back to
the same old phrase … *'it's only till you're back on
your feet'* … *'your life is temporary'* …

4 August 1978

We make beautiful music together. Harmonies float
back and forth. He is the words, I am the music, and he
plays me like an organ, pulling out all the stops so that
my whole being vibrates and I revel in the glory of it
all. I've become one of the Folk Club, accepted by
them, we've been camping together … not quite my
scene … but I'm fitting in. And there's this sense of
belonging. It's a new experience and I'm revelling in
every nuance, every sight, every sound, because it's all
so wonderfully new.

Tonight we've gone to bed early. We're still being careful, circling, testing, unsure … But then a loud, insistent knocking breaks the spell. I'm reminded of the telephone ringing that first night. This time someone is at the door. We try to ignore it, but it isn't going away. Our world is invaded, we're no longer alone. And then shadows pass under the window, whispered voices. I urge Melvyn to be careful.

'See what they want, but only open the door a crack. I've a funny feeling about this.'

My heart is pounding. Shivers are playing with my spine. This is not a neighbourhood where night visitors are welcome. I pad cautiously to the window as Melvyn shuts the front door. He's angry.

'Some stupid joker has tied a dog to the door handle.'

It makes me even more uneasy, the fact no-one is there. I peer into the darkness. Suddenly my world feels unsafe. It's slipping from under me.

And then … *whoosh*!

A brick lands through the window.

Glass flies in all directions. I duck my head, folding in on myself. *We're at war!!!!!!*

'It's okay, Jan. Take it easy. I'm calling the police.'

It isn't okay. It's Bill … he's found me … he's out for revenge. He knew I was leaving, but the threat was always there about seeking a divorce. He's out to get me. He's going to kill me this time. I can say things about him ... I know the way he is ... I'm a loose end he'll want to finish off ... finally ... completely ...

I'm cowed in a corner. I'll never be free of my past. I'm crying and I feel ashamed. I've brought this beast with me. It's not fair. Violence is all around me and within, I carry it with me everywhere I go.

'I'm sorry, my love. I'm sorry ... I'm sorry ... I'm sorry ...'

The police arrive, the atmosphere calms over hot sweet tea. There's been a spate of incidents in the area instigated by a group of West Indians. The all-clear is sounded, but I continue to cry. My thoughts aren't rational, and yet they make perfect sense to me. The police leave. Nothing they can do. They can't erase my past. Violence is as close to me as it always was ... a part of me ... a part of my life.

* * * *

Mum and Dad disagree with my new way of life. I've taken a job as a housekeeper as far as they're concerned.

'How can you do this?' they sigh. 'You're laying yourself wide open to get hurt all over again.'

Mum carries this sad look in her eyes. When we walk down the garden to greet her, hand in hand, she turns away ... shutting us out ... putting a barrier between.

My divorce hadn't come through and they can't accept another man in my life. To them, I've broken my wedding vows. I've walked away. Like the DSS, I'm a deserting wife. Beyond the pale. Bringing the family into disrepute. Even my sisters are stand-offish. They're doing things properly ... boyfriend ... engagement ... buying house ... wedding ... honeymoon ... kids ... and of course work and jobs and enough money ... and a family of their own. Meeting with any of the family remains strained. It's easier not to meet at all. It makes me guilty and upset ... *and I'm bad*!

'So how are things going?'

That look ... that pity ... that '*oh dear what are you doing with your life?*' Yes, I'm less than perfect. I'm right down there on the ground grovelling, pleading for them to like me, to accept me, to belong. Yes, I'm too sensitive. But ... well, it's just the way it is.

And I know I've made a mistake, using a solicitor who is a friend of my father, a respectable church-goer. Repeatedly he asks in reading the diaries of my past:

'Does your father know? What would he say? Do you want him to know? I think we'd best keep these things quiet, don't you?'

18 August 1978

People talk trivia around us. We try to join in, to become part of the crowd. It's a tea-party organised by Mum and Dad, but with their friends ... not ours There isn't anybody here that we know. I turn to the lady on my left to make a passing remark, to fill the aching silence. She turns away with a look as if she's just tasted something sour.

I lean towards a tray of food and, on impulse, deliberately upset a plate of neatly arranged cucumber sandwiches. It seems the signal between us for suppressed feelings to be released. We send cakes, puddings, pies flying in all directions. Once begun, it's contagious, we can't stop. At first people gathered around us are stilled, stunned, horrified ... shocked ... surprised ... disgusted at our lack of manners, our chaotic ways. But as they realise what we're doing, as tables turn, cloths stain brown with spilt tea, plates smash, chairs fall over, the careful and very polite tea party becomes bedlam, everyone clambering and talking and shouting at once. And we're running ... running ... running ...

A bedroom. A figure enters, the uninvited guest. The couple on the bed unravel. Melvyn makes for the window, dropping into the alley below. Mum gives chase. I follow in their wake, afraid of what she might do. We all three clatter through a maze of corridors. Mum is gaining on Melvyn ... she's right behind him ... but then ... I lose sight of them as they round the final corner. My breath is coming in short gasps. My legs almost give way. But I force them on ... on ... on ...

Mum stands alone.

'What have you done with him? Tell me ... tell me ... where is he? What have you done?'

She smiles contemptuously.

294

'Melvyn ... Melvyn ... Melvyn ...'

There's an empty space in my heart.

I wake from the nightmares, sweating, confused, not knowing where I am. Comforting arms hug me tight until I know I am safe.

'No-one will take you from me ... Promise.'

Melvyn is talking softly, silencing my fears.

'I promise, my darling, I will never leave you ... *never ...*'

23 August 1978

'Meet family in town for salad lunch. And yet I'm so emotionally withdrawn and restricted in their company I'm relieved to be gone. It's like I'm always wrong. And the guilt is killing me. It stops me being able to look them in the eye. Is it me? Is it them? I don't know any more. I just know I shouldn't feel this way with my own family. I'm not normal.

I'm being pressured, having to account for my actions, being judged. I continually withdraw from the conversation and sit on the sidelines, listening to other people's lives. I really can't find a way of fitting in. I don't belong. Choosing my words carefully, as if every step is a minefield, I wait on tenterhooks to see how they will be received. And then more often than not, find the conversation has moved sideways, like a crab, avoiding confrontation

295

and everything I've just said.

It's almost as if they feel I've passed the point of redemption. Every new thing I say or become involved in just adds fuel to an already roaring fire, confirming in their eyes I am a less-than, someone to be pitied, someone who needs direction, someone lost without a cause.

Christmas Day 1978

We've been busy with presents all morning, taking our time tucking into a huge turkey. It isn't until evening, when we turn off the TV ... yes, we have a TV now, we've joined the masses which he swore would never happen! ... that we find words amongst all the emotion of the day.

'If your decree absolute is confirmed as expected on 16th of next month we could be married by special licence on 18th.'

Was that a proposal? I savour the words, rolling them around my mouth like a favoured sweet.

'Was that a proposal?'

Wow! I mean ... *whoopee*! Happy ever afters can really exist then? Well, I'm about to find out.

Suddenly, I want to share ... to spread the word ... to include my family in my happiness. Surely this will turn them around?

(Oh stupid girl ... stupid naïve little girl ... you really haven't learned, have you?)

'Hello … Happy Christmas everyone!'

I'm shouting down the phone, hardly able to hold back, hoping … well, hoping …

'Are you all having a good time?'

I know my sisters and their respectives will be there. I'm the only one missing. Again, I'm already in the wrong.

'And what did Father Christmas bring you?'

I'm looking at my gifts piled high … no Christmas tree, no decorations because he needs to maintain his Leftist standards in not giving way to consumerism, convention-ism, commercialism … we'll overlook the Porsche sitting outside! Oh, and no knick-knacks … everything has to be The Best … The Most Expensive … High Quality … or else it means nothing at all. So the stocking filler plastic engine filled with bubble bath, the handkerchiefs embroidered with his initial, the gold chocolate pennies, the toothbrush and shaver … I recall his face on pulling each of them free … *disdain? Disinterest? What the … And where are the Boyz Toyz? Where is the computer gear? The software? The clickety-click merchandise which will make things happen at a touch?*

I still have so much to learn.

But then there's the Yamaha silver flute that is mine ... the over-large box of chocolates ... folk music to show me the way it's done ... and the right kind of music to play ... his kind of music ...

I'll get it right next year ... promise!

The family has lapsed into silence. I'm struggling to find words. Somehow I know the response isn't going to be what I need. Desperately, I want to convey to them ... what?

'I love you ... love you all. We wish we could be with you, but ...soon.'

It's coming to the point when the receiver will go down. I won't have shared.

'Mum ...'

'Yes ...'

I can almost hear it ... that barrier crashing down between us. And still I haven't said ...

'Mum ...'

Melvyn takes my hand into his own as I say, all in a rush:

'I've just been proposed to, and I'm so deliriously happy.'

We hold our breath.

'Please … please be happy for me?'

The child. She's come to the fore. I can hear her pitiful cry. Rising above all else, she's wanting … needing … acceptance … to know she is loved.

The phone crackles. I want to see Mum's face, to have her throw her arms around me, to know everything is okay. Yet, right now, I'm thankful of the space between.

'And did you accept?'

The words are whispered, as if she's half dreading my reply.

'Of course I did.'

I'm indignant. Why would they think not? Hushed hurried whispers are like mice the other end. Then Dad comes through, the voice of authority:

'Well, we'll leave it at that for now, Poppet. We'll be in touch soon.'

Melvyn doesn't drink. But given the occasion he produces a bottle of Bristol Cream, an attempt to put the sparkle back into Christmas.

Only later do I discover just how upset my parents really were at my news. It was a shock. *But didn't they see it coming?* They were remembering my first engagement … to Bill … how I displayed my ring proudly and without warning Christmas 1973 … taking it now as they had then … a sign of something bad … something about to break … something …

It crucified me inside to think they didn't understand.

Colour Me Carefully

'Advice is what we ask
when we already know the answer
... but wish we didn't

17 January 1979

It's somehow fitting that the date of my second marriage is to be 18 January 1979. My marriage to Bill had been 19 January. It's almost an eclipse ... the cancelling out of one by the other ... or so I like to think.

At the courts on the eve of the wedding we're given a cool reception by the lady on duty.

'Good morning. Can I help you?'

She is formal, not even the hint of a smile. After all, to her we're just another couple getting hitched. But I want the fanfare of trumpets, the clash of cymbals, a bugler to herald our new beginning. It's the end of tyranny and oppression and the start of a new kind of freedom. I've been granted my Decree Nisi, now I need a Decree Absolute to dissolve the marriage completely. I wish it was as easy to blank the past. To erase everything that had been done to me. To begin again, free of shadows ... free of fear.

'Ah yes, Mrs D … You'll have to wait a few minutes. There's been a mistake …'

The lady behind the desk looks a little ruffled.

'A mistake?'

My first thought is that Bill has chosen to contest at the last minute. That I'm never going to be free of the monster, never able to lead my own life. She disappears behind a partition, and comes back with a sheaf of forms. I clutch the desk for support, fearing the worst.

'I'm afraid this is going to take some time.'

She's prolonging the agony and I'm screaming loud and long in my head where it can't be heard.

'We have a few forms for you to fill in.'

She indicates with a stab of the pen where I should sign.

'Now Sections A, B, C, D, are correct. But we still need you to fill in the missing details of C.'

I oblige, expecting her any moment to say Bill is demanding me back. The prisoner is retained at her Majesty's Service …

'Right, that's about it, I think.'

She brings the stamp of officialdom with a firm flourish and hands me my papers. With a '*Next please …*' we are dismissed … I'm free to go … FREE!

18 January 1979

The Registry Office is like a Doctor's Waiting Room. We sit, huddled together, listening for the calling of our names. I feel drugged or drunk, disorientated, living walking in a dream, my divorce papers clutched tight to me. My passport to freedom. This is my happy ever after. I can't believe it's true. Then we're being led into the inner sanctum, to be clinically dealt with by the immaculately dressed man in charge. We answer his questions in hushed, nervous whispers, overawed by our surroundings and the vows we're about to commit to.

'Janine, will you take Melvyn Leslie Justin Totts to be your lawful wedded husband? Will you love him, comfort him, honour and keep him in sickness and in health, as long as you both shall live?'

The man's voice droned on. It sounds bored. As if he's said the words too many times already that morning. It's a solemn moment. But I wish he could look more alive, put some feeling into the proceedings. It reminds me of The Munsters ... Herman. He stands so stiff and formal, now waiting for my reply. A lady sits at his side, pen poised, ready to ink in details, to put the final seal of approval on our marriage. None of it's real. *What's the matter with me?* Suddenly, I can't remember how the hell I got here ... never mind who I'm about to become. *What's my name? Who am I?* My world is closing in on me ... shutting me down.

Melvyn's hand slips into mine.

'I look like a monkey in a suit, sticking out in all the wrong places,' he'd said at the start of the day. 'And I'll be nervous. You'll be able to hear my teeth chatter.'

'As long as you keep your leg still and don't let it quiver at the altar,' I'd bantered, recalling another wedding in another time, another place … eons of light years ago.

He'd not looked forward to the wedding. He didn't believe in such things, when it came right down to it. Again, his Leftist beliefs. On the bookshelf one day I'd found a little red book.

'That's my Marxist book … *'The Thoughts of Chairman Mao.'*

He'd held it like it was the Bible … and in a way it was … his Bible. He'd explained, but lost me in the first few sentences. I'd listened anyway. But … well … it was a different distant world to mine.

I fiddle with the emerald engagement ring on the third finger of my left hand, smoothing imaginary creases in my green velvet suit … Melvyn's choice. I wish it were a white wedding dress with a long lace train. It doesn't somehow fit the dream. And a church, not an office. Bridesmaids … bells ringing … bouquets … people cheering and happy and smiling and laughter all the way from the altar to a car waiting to whisk us off to a honeymoon.

Where are my parents?

Where are Melvyn's?

His father died years ago. His mother a devout Roman Catholic doesn't accept marriages in Registrar Offices. Any relatives … well, silence on that subject. I'm still probably a Housekeeper and beyond the pale. And no, my parents didn't come to the wedding. They had moved, just as they said they were going to. It was too much of a trek. We were going for a Blessing soon after. But otherwise, the day is ours alone.

'I will'.

The words are spoken … the deal done. *But who are the winners, and who the losers in this game of life*? Too early to know. Only two cards show for now …

Man and wife.

'Too late to back out now,' Melvyn's brother kids as we traipse out in single file.

'When are we going to eat?'

Melvyn's nieces are hungry. A restaurant just down the road has a table booked, bringing everyone together finally to celebrate and toast the occasion.

We pose for pictures on the steps outside. It's cold. The world walks past, uncaring. It's a cold blustery January day, and I pull up the collar of my fur against the cold.

24 January 1979
I'm a newly married wife. And yet, after only a few days of marriage, I find that little piece of paper called a

Marriage Certificate holding us together hasn't made any difference. The cracks still show ... the dreams, the guilt and everything that goes with them. Melvyn believes I need professional help. The time has come ... he says.

Our first session with the Analyst begins today.

'Word Association ... *Day*', I begin.

'*Night,*' responds Melvyn, logical as ever.

'*Black,*' I counter.

'*White.*'

'*Pain,*' my voice drops to a whisper.

'*Pain*?' queries my other half.

'*Pain.*'

'*Hurt,*' Melvyn continues on.

'*Bruised ...*'

My words are a whisper, Melvyn's loud brash word-statements ... crashing into the silence like church bells ringing from a tower. But then ... I'm crying. This isn't a game any more ... it's reality ... my reality ... and all the times I've been hurt I start feeling again. Melvyn tries desperately to change the subject, but it isn't going away. Every word he begins thereafter ends up exactly the same way ... back to violence ... back to past ... back to Bill and pain.

27 January 1979

We're getting to know our Analyst … I say 'our' Analyst, but the sessions are really centred around me. I'm the problem. I'm the one who needs help. Yes, I realise that now. There's always been something about me … something … He's a quietly spoken man who greets us each visit at the door of a very striking house, leading us through to his study. We sit comfortably in armchairs while he sits on a cushioned couch. He explains his role is Listener … and Melvyn expounds his theories, like evolution it takes forever …

I try to remain in the background, overawed, not really understanding a word.

Melvyn outlines our 'symptoms' … I have 'dreams', he says. I keep saying 'sorry' … *for goodness sake, it's only because I'm always in the wrong*! I have issues … issues? Yes, issues … such as suppressed anger. I won't take part in a discussion in case it ends in an argument and I might get hurt. Now that's totally illogical. I mean, how can words hurt? *Oh, but they can*! I have a total inability to see sense or reason. I don't understand simple commands. *Commands*! I'm timid and shy and choose to hold back, sitting in corners in cafes … my choice, but then again, *that's wrong*! I don't get technical, and keep hold of sentimental things. I talk in emotion. I have feelings that don't make sense. Oh, and then of course … the S word … I can't speak the S word … I can't cope with anything to do with the S word … and any simple straightforward everyday normal average positions I don't even know what to do with. *How is a man supposed to cope with a wife who can't be a proper wife*?

307

The Analyst moves on, asking what Melvyn's problems are.

Ah, I remain totally still, and very very silent. But wait … *he* doesn't have any problems. This is about *her. How dare the session start to concentrate on him! We're not here for him … we're here … for me. Doesn't the Analyst understand? Can't he see with his own eyes?* Melvyn's thoughts are clearly etched across his face.

Okay, just to play the game, go along with things …

But no … he doesn't want to hear from him … he wants to hear from me!

Me!

I can't say anything against him. There isn't anything to say. The silence lengthens. I look at the floor. Melvyn tries to interject, but is hushed. And so he continues looking at me … long and hard … their eyes penetrating my skin. I can feel them lifting the layers, reaching my thoughts, prising them out of me as a cook would an oyster. I cling to my shell … holding tight … until …

'I suppose there are things maybe … just a few …'

I look up then. Gauging the reaction. The Analyst is nodding approval … *but Melvyn?* He wonders what I will say.

'He maybe uses technicalities as a cover for shyness and embarrassment, to cover confusion, I guess. But then I might have got that completely wrong. It might not be that at all … and after all, it's not important in the scheme of things. Then again, he can switch off and go into a world of his own … is that all right, I mean, to say that?'

The Analyst is looking at me … searchingly. I shrug. Melvyn is quiet, distracted, I wonder what he might be thinking … whether he resents me sharing my thoughts.

The session only seems to last half an hour or so, and Melvyn is just getting into his stride, seeming to enjoy it, when the alarm clock goes off … we've gone over time. And next time? Well, he just wants to see me. I'm the more urgent. He'll come back to Melvyn at a later date.

That has me in a dither!

3 February 1979

We arrive at our second session prepared for just me going in, but then he wants to see both for personal details of birth, address, etc. Now he is saying he'll see us on a Saturday, but alternate, Melvyn next Saturday, me the one after, and he wants me to attend Tuesdays also … alone. Melvyn duly goes off into the next room.

But the Analyst remains still and silent. He doesn't speak at all … just keeps nodding, as if prompting me to speak. *What about*? I have no idea. He seems to break with his own tradition and explains that it is his role to listen … mine to speak. I should start in childhood. Then he's silent again.

I talk about the sheltered atmosphere in which I was brought up, centred around the church, and all the good things in life. It was a happy time as I recall, when I was left wondering if there might be more to life than the world I could see around me. Mum and Dad were reluctant to let me in on what the cruel bitter world outside was really all about. And I was left with the impression, like Red Riding Hood, that I should keep to paths they designate, rather than wander off to discover things on my own. They seemed to live in their own private world, letting no bad or evil penetrate, wanting me to only see good in people. It meant I wasn't prepared. They loved me too much to let me learn through my own experience, and tried to protect me … wrapping me in cotton wool, shielding me from harm, believing in The Church and The Family above all else. Ideally, I was sure they would have welcomed the chance to have me move on only as far as next door if we had to move at all … except Charlie somehow wasn't good enough. Twenty-eight or thirty was the age at which they expected me to marry, and then into a good Christian home.

The session comes to an abrupt halt with the sudden sharp shrill of the alarm. I'm getting into my stride, about to start sharing myself at the age of eight. But then later, when Melvyn and I go over what was said, I realise just how much I've missed. I've mentioned the hospital in passing, the fact I had to wear hospital shoes. I said nothing about callipers … green railings … a specialist beyond the dark green door … white coated figures … and fingers reaching … holding … hurting …

6 February 1979

It's like I'm going to the dentist this morning, I'm frayed around the edges, carrying this awesome feeling of dread. But then, perhaps it's because today is the first day I'm going alone to the Analyst. Memories we've stirred are churning inside. It's not easy to put them back in their box and close the lid. It's like they're saying *'I'm here, I'm challenging you to listen, to look, to learn ...'*

The Analyst likes to set a word as a starter and then shuts up for the rest of the session until the alarm goes and it's time to depart. A strange way of conducting counselling. With no feedback at all it's hard, as if I'm talking to myself with a stranger looking on. Today the word he sets is *'Different'*. I talk at length about how callipers made me feel compared to other children, how each time we moved I dreaded having to try to make friends and explain about my leg. Then I left school, only to have to restart again in order to be able to study music to 'A' level standard, in a class two years younger than myself.

I know I felt a failure, that I'd let Mum and Dad down, not getting either RE or Music qualifications. And this feeling continued until I married Bill against their wishes and it didn't work out. I'd always wanted to go to College instead of school. This above all else is the thing I regret not having done, because it was a turning point in my life. Out of the decision to go back to school came the music teacher abuse as well as Bill ... when everything could have been different. And all because I lacked the courage to stand up against my parents.

311

The remainder of this session we talk about my marriage to Bill. How life was about waiting on him, refusing to let rip or to stand my ground as anyone else might have done. Again ... *different*. In the end, I expected to be hit, abused, walked over, to have as little money as possible. It was the Norm. Then there was Kate and the trouble that followed.

The Analyst actually commented on how empty of feeling I am about events, of how I speak almost third person, as if I'm not affected. I manage a transference of the anger I should feel, the same as I do Melvyn. Then again, he believes my barriers stem from childhood and manifest themselves in marriage. He also points out that instead of thinking myself a failure, I should think on about how much my parents let me down.

10 February 1979
Today, finally I feel as if we're getting somewhere. It's more about emotion, how I feel rather than what happened.

We go back to that bedroom in the council house and I recall so vividly the empty feeling of being totally isolated and alone and vulnerable. I talk about the book I'm reading, and how much I identify with the heroine, a little innocent, who was never prepared for womanhood or how cruel and evil the world can be. The Analyst calls me simple and childlike in my ways ... not stupid ... not childish ... but *childlike* ... in how I view life and how much I want it to be built from the promises of childhood and unreal expectations given to me by my parents. He asks if I feel that way about

312

myself. And I wonder … remembering the shock of not finding the world this big beautiful place it had been built up to be. '*Good attracts evil*', he muses. Again I wonder.

I relate the experience of being kissed for the first time and spending the next six months thinking I'm pregnant. Each morning I'd look in the mirror, imagine I was growing, feeling so much bigger inside … something moving. I was so scared. And with no-one to talk about it, I felt so alone.

We talk for a long time, he as well as I for a change, about how Melvyn and I met. But more and more I'm feeling as if I'm having to justify my actions … to myself or to the Analyst, I'm not certain. And strange how a voice … my voice … keeps re-iterating how lucky I am to have lived and experienced so much. Those people I went out with before Melvyn seemed so shallow, so empty, as if they knew nothing about life … how it really was. Even though I was stuck in a rotting marriage for almost five years, I've seen more of life and got more out of my existence so far. Perhaps I'm not so wasted and downtrodden after all … or rather, perhaps this is the positive coming out of a very negative experience. Am I turning a corner? I maybe have a lot to be proud of after scraping myself up off the floor. Now I need to make something of myself before it's too late. Make the past work for me instead of against me.

We talk about how my role with Bill has been as a mother with a wayward child, rather than a wife. A child rebelling, switching anger against his mother … which I do feel was a very real thing for him at the

313

time. His mother abandoned and rejected him. I had taken her place. He held so much anger against her … against women in general.

More than anything else, the Analyst seemed to see me handing over control to another rather than reclaiming it as my own.

13 February 1979
I begin this session with the Analyst by describing the three very strange episodes I've experienced over the weekends.

The first took place in the kitchen. I swung around, surprised at an imaginary child's voice saying '*Mummy*'. The next incident took place in bed on Sunday morning. Melvyn had gone out to get some milk. The wind must have made the bedroom door open a little. I heard the same child's voice saying she wanted a cuddle and to give Daddy a surprise when he came back by hiding under the bedclothes. The final mysterious episode occurred on Sunday night as we were going out to the Folk Club. It was more of a conversation. I was telling the child that Mummy and Daddy were going out and she must be good for Aunty.

In each instance, I saw the child, certain of the beautiful head of curls. And her hair was auburn. And no, it wasn't me. It was a little girl.

I relate how Sunday evening was our first attempt at singing together in public. And while singing one of my songs 'April '78' all the feelings of the past welled up inside me and at the finish I was hard pushed not to burst out crying.

The Analyst listens now with a keen interest, commenting on how well I seem to be at hiding my true feelings below the surface. This in turn triggers off guilt at not being able to show love for Mum any more by hugs, kisses or terms of endearment. I stopped saying prayers with her at night when I was still a young child. I closed in on myself. I was choosing to do things alone. And it left me with a lasting impression that she felt I was lowering my standards which was definitely not the family way.

At the end of the session I make it clear that I don't condone or criticise any of my parents' actions. I was simply retelling incidents as I saw them. I love them both dearly. In response, the Analyst asked a question. *Have I ever told my parents to shut up, or stood up for myself against them?* I've never rebelled. I'm a good girl … and yet look where it got me! I've always put their feelings first, put my own aside for fear of hurting them. It's what you do, don't you? They're your parents.

His words remind me that when I first tried to leave Bill, it was their reaction that sent me back. I lived a further two years in violence. Then when finally I left it was about '*what will they think?*' '*How will they feel?*'

But … *it was my life*!

17 February 1979

I'm very disappointed and depressed. This session today hasn't gone well. I went into it with a very real sense of achievement. But then he sat in his chair in the usual way, with an aloof and indifferent expression, listening to me recount what happened at home.

I'd been moved by a TV programme about a young widow who, after her husband's tragic and untimely death, had remade her life with her young son. Her life ran parallel to my own. At first, she lived like a hermit, preferring her own company, refusing to answer the door to callers. Then she began to change her life by joining activities at her local Community Centre. She met a young man while out shopping one day. One thing led to another. And they married and she is pregnant.

The programme triggered a chain reaction of feeling, and I suddenly gagged as all the pain of the past I'd been trying so hard to ignore flooded through. Melvyn returned from work. We talked it out, and suddenly there were three separate accounts of happenings ... memories ... slipping out the black box in my mind ...

'It was a syrupy, gooey darkness, sweet like tea. I had a cup by the side of me which someone was trying to force on me. Mist turning to grey then white. But I just wanted to sleep, to be left alone ...'

The Analyst sat, unmoving in his chair. Other episodes followed. Perhaps I didn't want to remember. But when the session ended, I felt kind of lost, confused, upset. *Were the experiences important?* He didn't answer. Melvyn had made notes on what

316

happened. It presented another perspective. But he didn't want to know. And when he saw Melvyn alone he didn't even mention the subject.

I feel hurt and frustrated by his lack of communication and support. I want to know … for him to share his thoughts. After all, he's the professional!

Later, the two forgotten episodes return bringing an avalanche of feeling like a river suddenly breaking its banks …

'In bed … dark. A hand is moving over me. I move to my side of the bed. Movement becomes more urgent … grabbing … insistent. I feel pressured, stifled, pushing it away. Hand becomes cruel. Pinches nipples painfully. Moving down. Pain in lower regions … no, not wet! Nails bite in. If I cry out the hand will either clamp over my mouth, or else slap me hard. I feel every move it makes. Weighed down, there is more pain as he moves on top, asserting his Dominance. I cry out. Pause. 'Well, you'll do it anyway. It's about time.' All the time … dark … the furtive movements of a hand. Now impatient. 'Not again … please!' 'Yes, you'd better do it this time.' Thrusts. Not wet. I cringe. Cry out why is it always the same? Thrusts again because it will not go in. In, out … in, out. 'Why can't you be like other women?' Let it be over soon. I'm a failure, I know, so why not leave me in peace? No good as a woman, no good as a wife. Cannot keep my man happy. Then it is over. I am left to cry quietly, softly so as not to wake him or he will send me into the cold spare room for the remainder of the night. Left with the feeling that it's all my fault.'

The third darkness episode is, in my belief, myself coming round after being knocked out.

> 'From dark comes grey. Gradually I become aware of pain, particularly in my head. Not just aching, hurting. I feel bumps. I am lying on the floor by the side of the bed. I feel terrible. Can't think straight. My mind is a blank. What has happened over past hours? All I can think is that dinner needs to be cooked, washing up, rooms to tidy, beds to make. I try standing, but my legs are wobbly. I fall down. Each turn of my head brings new pain.

20 February 1979

Since leaving Bill I haven't been able to remember. Time is lost. All those years gone. Even childhood has betrayed me. I cannot reach back and find them. It is as if my life starts from this point, the point at which we met ... Melvyn and I.

And yet, like a car's headlamps picking up objects in the dark of night, I catch glimpses of happenings. Are they real? Did they happen to me? Is this the past which makes me so afraid? If so, do I really want to know? Do I need to know what happened?

Today is my final session with the Analyst.

The sessions leave me so confused, so desperate, so up-ended, Melvyn has decided they should stop. Perhaps our commitment to one another will see it through. I just need to settle. To know I won't be hurt. He is here for me now ... protecting ... guiding ... nurturing ... knowing what is best.

We go in together regardless of his rules and sit together, spending the time we have talking, sharing the way it is. The Analyst raises an eyebrow here and there. Then, as the clock rings the alarm, offers no words of instruction or advice … simply lets us go.

I'd been instructed by Melvyn to hand him a prepared letter at the start of the session, but he won't open it and refuses to comment. I try to explain how, on Saturday last, I felt inhibited by not having any encouragement or comeback leaving me confused and frustrated, feelings which didn't easily go away. I'm angry with him. He doesn't discuss what I share. *So what does it matter? What does he care? What's the point of the sessions?*

His response is that we expect too much. Our goals are unrealistic. It takes time before results might be seen. It seems like he would have us continue on … and on … and on … without anything ever changing at all.

But then, who is to say that he didn't begin the process of regression … my memories beginning to return? Who is to say that in some way what we were doing together was working?

We part on a friendly note … handing over £100 costs.

24 February 1979
Another episode grabs me. We've gone to bed early. I've just lain aside my magazine in preparation for sleep, when a noise at the door makes me jump. And then I'm back in a large empty bed. At some point in

the past I've woken to a similar noise and lain trying to convince myself it was all my imagination.

'The noise came again, distinct in the darkness. I froze. Darkness closing in on me, smothering, suffocating. Yet I can't move. My body paralysed with fear. A hand gropes in the darkness. Warm breath, the heat of another body closing down on mine. Contact! Panic! A hand grips, twists, hurts. Thrusting ... ramming ... hurting until my insides feel torn apart. My mind comes alive with pain. I can't think, only feel and hurt. I scream and writhe, trying hard to avoid the hand over my mouth. I am in agony, not knowing when it will end.

Bill. He hadn't gone to work, but to the pub returning home drunk. He stumbled about in darkness, then later come to bed lusting for action.

Much much later, I recalled the sequel. I had gone to sleep with the light on, and woken to see the door handle moving backwards ... then forwards ... then backwards again. Terror gripped me, but I was determined to overcome it. I closed my eyes, breathing deeply in an effort to compose myself, only to open them again a few seconds later. I burst out crying with relief ... Bill stood in the doorway. One of his sick practical jokes!'

I share with Melvyn. It's hard to make sense of things, knowing only they are cameos of a past filled with pain.

A Lasting Hold

To everything there is a season,
and a time to every purpose under the heaven;
a time to be born, and a time to die ...
a time to kill, and a time to heal;
a time to break down, and a time to build up,
a time to weep, and a time to laugh;
a time to mourn, and a time to dance ...
a time to keep, and a time to cast away ...

ECCLESIASTES, Chapter 3: 1-6

The evil sorcerer and the wicked witch are safely locked away. I throw away the key and begin to live without them. And yet ... their ghosts remain ... hauntingly familiar ... casting a shadow over today ... echoing my fears, my disillusionment, my pain. The nightmare lives on ... eternal.

Will I ever truly be free?

Little is said about the inner barriers that grow in a bad marriage. Mine were built over a period of ten years in abuse, violence and trust betrayed. But then the years that went before are also relevant ... including those at this time I can't recall. How long does it take to break open the secrets of the past? How long really does it take to be free? And what is freedom anyway?

What self-confidence I had has been whittled to almost nothing. And yet, perhaps, with Melvyn, I hope to begin to restructure, rebuild, put new plans in place for a different tomorrow. I am learning … to understand myself, to come to terms with the past and out of that to start the healing process.

But I can't help feeling I have left a part of my self behind.

Since the day I left Bill, I have never shown anger or said a cross word, or dared even think them. I still tense, ducking out the way of an expected blow. A raised voice creates panic and dread. I'm afraid of crowds and people. Often in the night I wake screaming from nightmares of beatings and rape.

There was a time when I resented my past coming between us, now I accept it as a part of me, a part of my past … present … future … it's the way things have to be. I can no longer blank it, or pretend it hasn't happened. As memories build, it takes only the slightest trigger to reduce me to a shaking wreck.

Just the other day, Melvyn was working late in his study. He had a tech problem on the computer. He was feeling the strain.

'Come to bed, love. Leave it till the morning.' I disturb his train of thought.

'Not now!' he snaps. 'Leave me alone!'

'I'll make coffee.' Still I linger in the doorway, loving him, unwilling to leave. Not wanting to be alone.

'Go away, Jan. Can't you see … I'm busy.'

I run then … run to the farthest corner of the house, cowering, head in hands. I hurt as if I've been dealt a physical blow. Tense, rigid with fear, my face twitches with fright. Images of the past slam down, thrusting me back to places I don't want to go.

It takes Melvyn a good half hour and then some to coax me back. Even then, I feel insecure, unsure. I shy away from him. No longer safe. It happens all the time. My past is a part of me and will not let me go.

But right here, right now, helping to obliterate my past, bit by crazy bit, is my daughter. She clamours now for attention.

'Mummy … Mummy … Mummy,' she murmurs.

She screams excitedly and I push my diaries and writings to one side, stepping out of darkness, celebrating the warmth, the light.

It took a year of false hopes, a series of tests, and an operation to remove the physical scars Bill left me before the way was clear to have a child. Just one. She is the missing piece of my puzzle.

She is my happy ever after.

The picture is complete.

I am fulfilled.

And yet how can you know if a story is complete?

Angel Meets Devil

*Never pretend to a love which you do not actually feel,
for love is not ours to command.*

'But what are we going to do?'

'I don't know … it means we're all of us homeless.'

'He can't do that … I mean, it's just not the way things should be.'

'I'll tackle him about it. I'm not afraid of him the way you are. Besides, someone has to bring all this out into the open. Someone needs to speak their mind. It's not going to go away … it's only going to get worse. It's what happens when good meets evil … when the Angel meets the Devil.'

It's a round table conference. For once in my life I'm not alone. This crisis is touching a family. My family. Every one of us is affected. Whatever the outcome, it is going to culminate in a life change.

The day before, Melvyn had been seen cavorting in the garden with a young woman … no-one knew who she was. She suddenly appeared with him. For weeks, more and more perfumed mail was arriving through the letterbox. Our daughter was picking them up: '*Phew! Daddy's letters smell funny … lavender …*' He'd become secretive, dropped weight, dressing in clothes we never even knew he had. A phone call from a hotel confirming bookings in his name left us wondering. He'd invested in a Toyota MR2 brilliant red ... his *'calling card'*.

Mum and Dad were increasingly worried at the bizarre behaviour of their son-in-law. They retired to live with us. I found them in shock on returning from a shopping trip, pointing down the garden, talking about Melvyn and the woman he'd been 'fawning' at his side. I got back in the car, determined to confront him. But I never reached Dowty where he was working ... at the roundabout before entering the estate I had a major car accident and had to come home. Melvyn didn't return that evening.

This morning, we've already had an Agency at the door demanding my bank card. I refused. He would be back. He had instructions. I telephoned the bank. They'd frozen the account. No money. Just like that.

This visit was quickly followed by another. When the door went and Mum answered, a man stepped past and on into the hall, writing copious notes on a clipboard, without invitation going through into my parents' room, the kitchen, the lounge, heading towards the stairs.

'*Erm* ... Excuse me young Sir, who are you and what d'you think you're doing?'

Mum's voice was demanding. Dad and I looked on in awe.

'Instructions from the owner.'

He'd continued towards the stairs, but Mum blocked his path.

'I rather think you are exceeding your authority and don't have the full facts. My daughter here is joint owner of this property. You certainly don't have her authority. And we are living here also. You don't have ours.'

The man's steps faltered. He looked at me uncertain, looked at her, at my father in the background, and then his notes.

'Well, I need to fulfil my obligation, to complete my inventory, and then I'll be done.'

His foot fell on the first stair. Mum held open the front door.

'I think you should go now before we call the police.'

He was gone in moments. But as the latest in a series of bizarre episodes, it left us shaken.

'He's trying to sell the house from under us!'

It didn't take rocket science to work that out. So what were we going to do? And again, that phrase:

'It's what happens when the Angel meets the Devil.'

When Melvyn put in an appearance, finally, grating his key in the front door lock, heading purposefully for the kitchen to make a hot strong coffee, Mum moved forward to tackle him.

'Melvyn, we need to talk. Never mind that. In here … *now*!'

She had on her no-nonsense voice, and he immediately dived for cover in the loo under the stairs. We could hear him on the phone. But he had to come out sometime. We knew that once he escaped out the front door we'd never pin him down. He'd an office purpose built next door which remained locked. It was in there he dealt with business, picking up his post, ferreting secrets away. Nothing he did made any sense any more. And he wasn't about to share.

Dad shrank into his armchair in their room. I sat in a hard backed chair the opposite side of the table to Mum, hidden behind a magazine. A hard knot of fear gathered in the pit of my stomach. Mum tapped her pen on the table top impatiently, making sure it was heard.

'Melvyn … we're waiting.'

Finally, he came out of the loo opposite the open doorway.

'Melvyn …'

'Right, I'm here, I'm busy, on a tight schedule. Make it quick. My time is money.'

'Sit down.'

Amazingly, he obeyed, sitting on the edge of a chair nearest the door. He was like a panther about to pounce … at his most dangerous.

For the next half an hour, for as long as he would sit there, Mum outlined the peculiar episodes happening around us, demanding an explanation, given that we were all equal members of the household and had a right to be included in any outcomes, certainly in being kept informed … especially if the house was being sold.

He quoted figures fast and furious. Money was what life came down to. It was all that mattered in the end. His father had gone bankrupt in his growing years, it was his breaking point, and he was determined the same would not happen to him. To everything else being thrown at him, he simply shrugged. He didn't care. He wouldn't get involved.

Finally, Mum made a bargain:

'Right, well if that's your attitude, and you're determined to pursue this path, then I'm sure your women friends aren't going to do your washing for you. I will do it, at a price. You say your time is worth £50 per hour. Those are my rates … you leave your washing with me and I will do it for the princely sum of £50 a time. You don't know how to use a washing machine. You need nice clean clothes for your impending dates. So why not humour me? What have you to lose? It's a business deal, that's all.'

He agreed … immediately handed over £50, almost running out the door and up the stairs, returning with more than one load of washing which he deposited in a heap in the kitchen. Then he left the house. The car revved away, down the road out of sight.

Mum gave me the £50 and told me to buy food for myself and my daughter. We'll keep it separate. Just in case. When you do a deal with the Devil, you need to watch your back!

But then, how did we ever come to this?

*   *   *   *

If I had remained a victim, unable to say 'No' or to speak up for myself, I have no doubt I would still be married to Melvyn now. It was the way I had to be ... he the Dominant, me the submissive, at all times. He in total control ... always.

We lived this way for years. Until the birth of my first book ... *A Crying Game*. Letters from readers followed its publication. And I founded LIFELINE as a country-wide network of support for families with violence in the home. It became a national registered charity recognised as an authority on abuse. Through the following years, I was taking part in all kinds of media interviews and programmes.

Knowing I wasn't alone, knowing it wasn't just me, had a profound effect. Suddenly it meant I couldn't be blamed any more for everything that was wrong. I wanted respect, to be treated as an equal, no longer needing to ask permission for everything, and be grateful for what I was given as if I had to earn it with good behaviour towards my husband ... like a good little girl.

I was commissioned to write two further books by Thorsons (now HarperCollins) which were published in 1988 and 1989, '*Behind Closed Doors: An Advice Book for families in abuse*', 1988, and '*Home is Where the Hurt Is: Surviving Child Sexual Abuse*', *1989*.

Memories were returning. I now knew I was a survivor not just as a battered wife, but also from child sexual abuse. It took over ten years of the right kind of therapy with a Clinical Psychologist, filling in the blanks, right back to my final memory ... my first abuse by the specialist at the hospital where I went for treatment with my 'club' foot. Understanding what happened to me as an adult rather than as a child made a difference. It made me question. I wanted to know, to blast secrets of the past. More than anything, I had to change my response so the same never happened again. And in sharing my experiences I was helping others, making good come out of all that bad.

I became accepted as a Consultant on Abuse, talking and sharing openly to help professionals and charities understand what it is to live through such experiences, and how they can best help others in that situation. I wrote articles, instigated surveys to prove the extent of the problem in the UK, created and led teaching workshops to challenge current thinking, speaking at conferences, and working at both ends of the problem ... with abusers as well as abused. Working with offenders and paedophiles meant learning from them exactly how they target victims and especially children, to better understand the problem as a whole and set up more effective child protection programmes for the future. Through LIFELINE we also set up self help groups for victims, then survivor groups, and also offender groups with set targets and achievements they had to realise. Those who didn't comply went straight to prison. I was involved in writing reports for the courts, visiting inmates at special secure units and prisons.

A 24 hour helpline went from our home. Often I was travelling to different parts of the country, involved in training, or calling on individuals desperate to talk, supporting, enabling, acting as a positive role model to offer hope where there was none.

* * * *

We were living in the Hebrides when my first book came out. I never saw my books sitting on bookshelves. We moved there when Melvyn discovered how cheap housing was on the islands after a family holiday in Scotland, the first after my little miracle was born.

It was idyllic, a wonderful way to bring up a child. My sister moved to live with us. I'd had major surgery after my daughter was born and couldn't lift her, so Mum and my sister's help was invaluable. However, once we moved, Melvyn went to work in the south of England and we rarely saw anything of him. Years on, I shared my concern with him that our daughter didn't have a father, at least not one she knew. We needed to become a family, to live together. I had effectively become a single parent. Added to which, she wasn't well. With severe asthma and the island built on a bog, it was only getting worse. I was afraid for her every time she caught an infection or cold. I'd have to carry her around like a bundle of rags, she was so weak. She was taking more and more time off school … and the situation was so serious I was communicating with Princess Margaret Hospital in Swindon. With no hospital on the island, it would mean in an emergency, a lifeboat or helicopter having to fetch us.

Eventually, my voice was heard. Melvyn and I took a couple of weeks of his very valuable time to identify a house somewhere in easy access of work. We'd stayed with him over the previous Christmas and got a taste for the mainland, for shops, for easy access and communication, and for being together in a way like never before. But he had to choose the house … it had to be his decision … finally he put in an offer on one in the country. *Why did we need one this big, with so much ground?* It would take so much upkeep. *Would he stay or be forced back into work elsewhere, and the same situation as we'd had in the Hebrides present itself over again?*

His response was to invite my parents to retire and live with us … which they did. At which point he arranged for a building in the grounds adjacent to the main house where all his technology went. It was like he was breeding machines, new ones appeared almost overnight. I had no idea what most of them were for, what they were capable of, why so many, but I knew they were expensive. And yet, like many wives who stay home and bring up children, supporting their husbands … home-makers … I trusted him to do the best by us, to keep us safe, to do the right thing.

It was only when we were living together finally as a family that the bizarre behaviour began.

Or perhaps it was that it was always there, but that I changed, and came to understand and see what I could not before?

We stopped having sexual relations because of what he wanted me to do. He classed himself 'A' sexual, which basically meant 'anything goes'. We took to separate beds in separate rooms. Somehow it was my fault given he was snoring ... but I had long given up trying to make logic out of a blame game. It was easier simply to agree with the status quo.

When it came to holidays, he didn't believe in them. Holidays were a waste of time. No-one would be paying for his time. As a workaholic, he could cheerfully work right through day and night and day, almost non-stop. Computers are addictive. I had no idea what else he might be doing closeted behind the doors of his own office effectively living next door.

He played mind games. In the days when I was subjugated into the mindset, I accepted everything at face value. It was like being a jelly in a mould. I gave up what I believed in ... my dreams, the way I did things, my music, my interests, fashion, everything that made me, adjusting and adapting so that it fitted with what he held to be true and right. It happened over time ... from the moment I left my past life as a battered wife, as a cardboard cut-out I was malleable enough to be honed to his will. He took control ... just like that. It's so difficult to explain how it happens unless you've been there. In the end, he could make me think black was white. That night was day. Things happened in the way he said they did, or they didn't happen at all.

But through the years, as I began to grow strong, to question rather than simply accept, it was as if he upped the ante, tightening the boundaries around my world. I thought I was going mad. During shopping visits, he'd be there right by our side one minute ... and then gone the next, completely without warning. Hours later, he would turn up, saying he'd been there all the time and he didn't know what I was talking about.

Was it him ... was it me ...?

Our daughter was nine years old when we shared our final holiday together. We took my sister's eldest son with us. And all was fine. It was just so good being together. We left Mum and Dad enjoying the peace of the house on their own. But then, we paid a visit for the day to Watermouth Castle in Devon. He was there as we entered, right there with us, looking at the fountains, and then ... gone!

I spent the day with the youngsters, but more and more a raging migraine took over my head. *What was happening? Was it me? Was I ill? Would he appear suddenly and say he'd been with us all the time as he usually did?* I should be well used to it. But as the day wore on, I became more and more worried. Finally, as evening came, they were locking up, still he couldn't be found. This time, we didn't have transport back to where we were staying. We were stuck in the middle of nowhere. The youngsters were tired. They wanted to leave. We'd seen and done everything twice, three times. They were bored.

We sat at the very top of the layers and layers of garden. I couldn't move with the pain. I'd lost my vision almost completely. My right side was weak. I felt like I was having a stroke. Even the children were concerned. They said I had gone pale, then grey. And the pain had taken over my body.

And then, out the corner of my eye, I saw him ... standing right there, watching us.

Or was he? Was I slowly going mad?

Yes, he'd been spotted by our daughter and he came to us then ... *but he didn't know what we were talking about! He hadn't been away. We'd just shared a lovely day together. Now it was time to go.* I was being accused of twisting minds against him. We went back to the place where we were staying ... and he left ... for home.

I have no idea to this day what it was all about.

Was he ill? Was I? Was it the games he got off playing? Was he really trying to drive me insane?

Bizarrely I began to wish he would hit me rather than mess with my mind. At least there would be a mark to show for it, to say what was happening, what he had done.

I was reminded of the old black and white film 'Gaslight' where a husband tries to make his wife believe she is mad. It's a strange feeling. To this day, I need to know if something is real, tangible, and I'm not dreaming or imagining it. I'm never certain. It's too easy still to simply believe something isn't really there at all.

His father had been diagnosed with schizophrenia. His brother had the illness and swore he would never have children and risk passing on the illness to them. There was every chance Melvyn had the illness according to a doctor I consulted. *But God help anyone who tried to say anything that might besmirch his good name!* And so we kept silent. It wasn't up for discussion. And I used '*Schizophrenia Fellowship*' as a support. Facts were important as was understanding, listening, support. The behaviour could be a result of the illness caused by stress.

What stress? What was really going on?

It was a shock to learn about schizophrenia. My psychologist, who worked with me fifteen years on and off; said he was a sociopath given he had no conscience. It made for a lethal combination. First time around I married a psychopath, someone who hyped on another's pain. The second time I married a schizophrenic/sociopath.

Whew! Stupid stupid me ...

But then, how do you know in the beginning? Everyone puts their best face on when they're dating. Now that skeleton was out the cupboard, it begged the question: *how much of his behaviour was a result of his illness, how much a part of his personality? And then again, how much was deliberate, done simply because he could, getting pleasure out of seeing me hurt ... keeping me in the role of victim?*

* * * *

The final episode came at the end of that year.

I'm invited to Malta, to work with authorities in a country where divorce is not an option. What can families do when there is abuse in the home? My first time abroad, and I'm to lead a seminar … something I've been doing in this country and welcome the chance to widen understanding, working with professionals about what it's like the other side of the table. But then as things get underway, I realise with trepidation, this is an open air seminar in the country's capital Valetta, in front of the largest hotel. The aim is to bring out the problem for the first time from behind closed doors to show it as an issue to be addressed. The media takes it up big time. It is plastered all over Maltese television and newspapers. Armed guards circle me as a form of protection. And I start to realise just how much of a challenge this is. But then, women hesitantly come out, begin to talk, to share, filled with nervous energy and courage, standing beside me, holding tight my hand, speaking in Maltese to involve and include me.

We spend Christmas with a lovely Maltese couple. Melvyn goes home early. He doesn't like the country. We return to celebrate New Year. But after my parents have gone to bed, suddenly, he raises his glass:

'And this is to toast 1990 … and a change in our contract of marriage.'

Fine … whatever … another strange game we're entering into! We go to bed. But soon after, an avalanche of post starts arriving. He's advertising in Forum Magazine. He's seen out with young women … and one comes into the garden, canoodling with him.

I make an appointment with a solicitor. I need to know where I stand, what I can do to stop the bizarre behaviour and repair our marriage. A letter duly arrives warning Melvyn to desist or further action will follow. His response is swift and immediate … and cruel. Everything is his … the house, the grounds, the cars, computers, furniture, everything we own … *right down to our daughter.* If I persist in my current course of action or try to effect change, he will put me and my parents back in the gutter where we belong, and take my daughter where I will never find her. I've always failed him, it seems, always been *'Second Hand Rose'.* I flunked all the tests put before me when we first met.

Suddenly, things start to make sense. I'm seeing our relationship and marriage in a very different light.

It is the solicitor who first says the word *'Divorce'.* *No! Not again, I can't divorce again. This is forever,* I want to scream. We have a home, a family and … what will happen to my parents? No, I just need you to make the pain go away, to bring back 'happy-ever-after'.

But then, the bank shuts down on me. I am no longer recognised on the account or able to get monies. The main branch and then head office in London insists no-one is available. DSS won't help. I have a home. I need to continue paying the mortgage or I will lose it. Red letters come through the letterbox. He's refusing to pay bills. To upkeep our home. He's withdrawn completely all support. An Estate Agent arrives to value the property. A Debt Collector threatens on our doorstep.

Life is a nightmare. We don't know what will happen next. Food runs out, our most basic need. My parents can't cope with the strain, nor with maintaining themselves and us. I know, however much I don't want it, that this is the end. I can't stop the trail of destruction that daily is getting worse.

Finally, a pen is carefully pushed in my hand as I sleep trying to make my signature, forcing me to sign everything over, my daughter included. *The final straw*!

As my parents and I sit down for yet another Council of War ... the phone rings. The minister who married my parents in 1950 has just died. The minister's wife is asking Dad to come out of retirement and take a part time ministry, moving into the tied house that goes with the chapel. It is the answer to a prayer. But they won't leave until they knew I'm safe. Melvyn has talked a lot about taking his daughter where I will never find her. He is capable of anything. We believe him to be a very dangerous man.

On 1st April I resign from LIFELINE.

It hurts like crazy to leave my friends behind. It was my lifeline also ... the one thing which supported and gave me life.

On 1st July I take my daughter to live in Malta.

As the only country in the world where the parent who takes a child in has to be the parent to take the child out, it is the only way. And ironically, the last person I helped on LIFELINE in turn helps me, buying my car, taking us to the airport to begin a new life. It is the only money we have.

Again, I am leaving everything behind.

I take a position at a Language School teaching English as a foreign language. At the same time I work with Social Services. People back home think I've done a *'Shirley Valentine'*. But life is crazy … it's damned hard work! Temperatures soar. I suffer a complete breakdown. But I need to keep money coming in. The couple we're staying with finds us a house to give us independence and we rent it, creating a new life.

For weeks, then months, we are happy.

We are free!

Or are we just kidding ourselves? Nothing is really settled. It's all put on hold until we return home.

My daughter is reading *'The Diary of Anne Frank'*. It seems appropriate. We are refugees, fleeing a war torn country, seeking sanctuary. Mum and Dad move one week after we leave and, aged 72 and 74 years old respectively, take up a new ministry. We keep in touch almost daily, by letter, by phone.

But then …

The Kuwait war happens! The unexpected …

Work ceases at the port, one of the main industries on Malta. English people living in the Maltese quarter aren't safe. We are advised to leave. I have no option but to book a flight, storing our belongings in a crate on a ship in the port, and we leave the white sands and blue clear waters of the Mediterranean, for the uncertainty of England.

We stay with my parents, knowing it isn't permanent. Melvyn has changed all locks on our home. Rumours are rife in the village about his lifestyle. We don't have a car. All we have is what we stand up in. There seems no way forward, no way back.

Stalemate.

Finally I apply to the courts for access to our home, knowing we can't afford to live there or pay the mortgage. And from that point in time, Melvyn disappears. He simply walks away from the mess and debt he has created, out of our lives, to make a new life elsewhere. It is impossible to make plans.

Ultimately, our beautiful home is repossessed. I literally beg a local farmer to rent one of his farm cottages long-term. We live up the back of beyond, collecting wood in the winter to make a fire to keep warm. It is basic ... but it's home. And we live there the next six years.

The divorce takes over a year, but finally I win on the grounds of '*unreasonable behaviour*'. Victory however, is bitter-sweet. I need to take Jo to school even as a teenager to protect her. I can't get work. We lead a frugal lifestyle. It isn't what I would have chosen ... but we adjust to a different kind of Norm ... and life moves on.

Colour Me with Love

Forgiving is not forgetting
It is remembering ... and letting go

This has not been an easy book to write for all kinds of reasons.

Will readers simply see me as a pathetic individual who brought much of the trouble upon herself? That is certainly how it feels at the time. *'It's all my fault'* becomes a recurring theme. It's the reason that control is so effective ... keeping someone ignorant, naïve, vulnerable, without understanding what is really going on, making them dependant, creating secrets with an implied threat attached to them. All are hidden aspects of abuse which become the rules by which a victim lives her life.

Writing this book has meant stepping outside the box ... outside my Norm. At first I was fearful, even all these years on. Only someone who has lived in control could perhaps understand that fully. But it became a necessary step for me today ... a step towards freedom and independence and accepting myself ... in finally clawing back control ... knowing I can without fear of punishment and reprisals.

Breaking taboos is never easy. It takes courage ... and those who have given me that courage are people I am meeting today who see themselves as victims, accepting what they have as a way of life, a life sentence. They ask the same questions I asked all those years ago … people who live in uncertainty, who have to find their own kind of courage to create a new life.

The most important question to ask is this: '*How did your upbringing inform the person you are today?*' There are no easy answers, and it isn't a blame game. But it does mean stepping back into the past to find out just how far you need to go to develop. Otherwise, you only have half the story, and you're not dealing with or understanding the whole.

A trip back into the past can be a cathartic experience. It enables you to see the person as you were then and the things that you would change. It empowers you to realise your full potential. For me, completing this book is like closure finally, drawing a line, opening all the secrets in all the boxes and just letting them go where they can do no more harm. A truly liberating experience.

There is no real ending to my story. It just helps to accept what happened as a necessary part of my learning process.

There are days when I wonder what I might say to the person I was in all the lives I led while qualifying for my PhD in Life.

In 1959 at the age of six years old, I spoke the words: '*He hurts me*', about the specialist at the hospital. It was a simple way of telling, of breaking the stranglehold of control and the secrets surrounding our visits. My mother thought enough of it to write those words in her diary. But nothing was ever said or done. The visits and the abuse continued … until at fourteen years old I went on strike and refused, no matter what the punishment, that I would never go back to the hospital again.

Where did that strength come from?

Where did that strength go when I needed it in the years to come?

Abuse wasn't talked about in the 1950s. It didn't make news like it does today. Abuse wasn't a word people used. People thought nothing of a child seeing a doctor alone. There was the trust, the honesty, the respect placed in people in authority. They would do no harm. It certainly never entered my parents' heads that anything was happening out of the ordinary. And for them, authority could never be questioned. Authority was always right!

And yet …

Early behaviour at the bottom of the garden with Charlie demonstrated I was trying to understand … through play. It wasn't Doctors and Nurses I was playing, but Doctors and *Patients*. Nobody asked why.

At school, why did I wear six pairs of underpants? Why was I so desperate to hide and protect my private parts? When we went to the doctor it was obvious something was wrong. Hysteria outside the gates was enough to illustrate the very real phobia and panic and upset it caused, not to mention the nightmares that followed after.

It's sad that it had to stay hidden all through the years. It wasn't until I was in my forties that finally I shared the secret with my parents.

Some victims never share. Never tell. For them it becomes a lifetime issue from which there is no escape. I was at the bedside of a woman in her eighties. She had never spoken about what happened as a child, but needed to before she died, desperate to know it wasn't her fault. In my case, maybe it was selfish, but I didn't want my parents to die without knowing the real me. And so one day I visited, we talked, we sat around the table and over a pot of tea I told them the way my life had been. Mum cried, desperately clinging to a photograph of when I was young. She needed to believe her daughter remained unsullied. It was as if the person sitting next to her was a stranger. My father was so angry. Red face, pressed lips, hardly able to speak. I asked him who was he angry at. And he said: *'You ... It means you've lied about your life, you were never honest, and look at what you've done to your Mum.'*

So ... *back to being my fault then!*

For the rest of his life, my father never spoke or asked me questions about the abuse or what had happened. He didn't want to know the truth. Neither would he hug or touch me easily again. It was as if I was contaminated. A barrier shut down between us. He couldn't cope with what had happened, many men can't. I don't know if he ever read my books. Did he even discuss the issues with Mum?

Mum felt guilt. She did everything she could to read up on the subject, to know how to support and to be there for me. We talked it through, right back to when I was a small child, and agreed the abuse at hospital had to have started around four years old, when she was pregnant with my sister. Prior to that, she always went in with me. Finally she accepted the truth. And she went on to work as a counsellor on LIFELINE with me and had her own clients, those who saw in her their Mum they couldn't talk to, their grandmother with whom they wished they might share. We became Soulmates because of the sharing. But she also said that had I told when I was a child, it would have split the family. And she was glad I had protected them from that by not telling my secrets.

And for me, that's the saddest part of all ... that the burden remains the child's alone.

In 1959, at the age of nine years old, my father went into the ministry and life changed forever, including my identity. My early years spent in the south of England became a never ending saga of moves, always watching for the packing cases as an early warning system, dreading having to make new friends.

Ten years on, just as we moved for the fifth time, I was targeted not just by the boys at the local youth club who took a bet to see how long it took to lay a minister's daughter and hence my soon-after rape; but by a music teacher. This remains an open case, waiting for other victims of that same music teacher to come forward, to name him as their abuser. He's been arrested five and six times. I made a statement, sketched places that mattered. I don't know what urged me in my early fifties to go to my local police station and open the secret of his abuse. But thank God it was taken seriously! For the next few months I was visited by CID, collecting evidence despite it happening all those years ago.

'What do you want to come out of this?' they asked.

'If others come forward, he would go to prison and never come out.'

'I just want him to acknowledge what he did all those years ago ... that's all.'

He doesn't even have to say sorry. Sorry would be meaningless. I just need him to say it happened, as we both know it did ... to acknowledge the truth. That's important to me. Because in all the years of his abuse, he never spoke about what he was really doing. He covered his actions by talking about something else, hiding behind a cloak of respectability.

In 1979 I married Melvyn. I'd been a battered wife/battered girlfriend for ten years. This was my happy-ever-after ending. But ... out of the frying pan into the fire. It became mental/emotional abuse. Far more than being beaten, it is soul destroying when someone tries to make you believe you are mad. You doubt reality. When someone plays mind games, they are messing with your head. And that is evil. You can never totally shake that kind of betrayal of trust. It is there always at the back of your mind ... *What if ...? How ...? Where ...?* begging clarification.

Like the specialist in the hospital, like the music teacher, he never talked about or discussed what was happening. *'I don't know what you mean?'* became the standard answer. Everything I'd shared so openly, so trustingly about past abuse was suddenly being used against me. Self harm returned. The bulimia and anorexic tendencies. I had no control over any aspect of my life. Until finally, all my feelings of self worth, all my confidence, all my dreams were snatched from me and rubbished, just as if they'd never been. Worst of all, he made me appear stupid and weak, inadequate and a failure as a mother to my daughter.

In 1989 it was the end of my marriage. The following year we lost everything and had to start our life over, just we two, my daughter and I.

Ten years on, my daughter had left home. I changed my name as did she by deed poll. It seems we both needed to cut ties with the past. I was living in a new place, and had just taken on a mortgage, working full time, driving my own car. These were things I'd been told as a child I could never do. *'You must live within your limitations'* were the words I grew up with, with a shake of the head, a sad look in the eye. But then, here I was, a part of the big wide world outside. ... living as an equal.

In 2009 I had a breakdown. It was the fourth breakdown of my life. But I was determined I wasn't going to have to start my life again. I wasn't going to be made homeless. After a few false starts, I'd been in a long term relationship lasting years. But then, slowly, I found he was lying to me ... truths kept creeping out of corners. He was married. He had a home. I took him back a few times … but he kept returning. And then one day he simply walked out and never returned. There was no warning of his leaving. And the worst of it was, with no contact, I thought he'd had an accident and died. But then he started texting, saying he was coming back with no intention of doing so … having walked away to live his dream with a younger woman.

It was April the following year, 2010, I met the man who ulatimately changed my life. Everything we do together is *more than* because of the past, many things even '*a first*'. He's been on a deep learning curve ever since … yet somehow, he understands. He is there for me … protecting, guiding, learning, teaching, nurturing as we shape a new future together.

I love him so much. We are equal. That is something very new. He listens … what I say and share matters. We discuss everything to ensure he understands. It is because of him that I am able to look back into the past with fresh eyes … remembering … letting go.

It is time to put the record straight, to tell the real story behind the story, filling in the gaps, restoring memories which returned and which make me whole.

My first book published in 1984: '*A Crying Game – The Diary of a Battered Wife*' was the only experience I remembered at the time. And yet there is so much more as this book lays testimony.

To anyone reading this today who shares any part of my experience, I would say this. Please know you are not alone. That is so important. There are so many thousands upon thousands of souls who are being hurt today in their own home – physically, mentally, emotionally, sexually - across the world.

Be warned, there are long term effects. Because of past persistent beatings to my back, neck and head, I have ongoing chronic pain and am disabled, with the most horrendous head pain lasting days they haven't yet found a painkiller to combat effectively. I also have Post Traumatic Stress. Everyday things can trigger me back into the past and it feels just as if it is happening again today for real. This in turn causes 'Fugues' … times when I simply disappear into myself, switch off from the present, losing minutes, hours, even a whole day if it's bad enough before I come back to being the person I am now. I know it must have been what I did as a child, on returning home from hospital. It's the reason I couldn't remember.

Remember, if you stay, domestic violence will only ever get worse. Abuse is an escalating cycle. It goes on to affect every aspect of your life. And yet, you have the right to live free … to love and to be loved … to be accepted just the way you are. I promise you, it's a wonderful way to be!

Love is out there … true love, that is … a love that is so vital, so energised, so pure, so genuine and real that one day it is going to gather you in its arms and say:

'You have arrived! This is the beginning of the rest of your life … enjoy!'

Isn't it worth taking that chance?

BOOKS

Published in the name of Janine Turner

- *A Crying Game – The Diary of a Battered Wife*, Mainstream, 1984
- *Behind Closed Doors – An Advice Book for Families with Violence in the Home,* Thorsons (now HarperCollins), 1988
- *Home is Where the Hurt Is – Surviving Sexual Abuse,* Thorsons (now HarperCollins), 1989

Still available through Amazon

Published in the name of Janine Harrington

- *Nina & Vic: A World War II Love Story,* Woodfield, 2004

  My mother's wartime story sharing the journey of two ordinary people set against the backdrop of war, and a man flying ops in a secret group, identifying and jamming enemy radar.

  Janine is a founder member and Secretary of the worldwide RAF 100 Group Association, and Editor of their magazine 'Confound & Destroy'.

- *Secrets of the Grimoire: The First in a Trilogy of the Enchanted Kingdom of Paragon,* Nightingale, 2008

A fantasy for the older child, set in Yorkshire, about Paragon, a perfect kingdom and how good always attracts evil ... and the war against the elements to protect all that is good and whole and pure.

- *Brothers: A World War I Story of Courage & Commitment,* Farthings, 2010

  The story of my two great uncles, Will and Arthur, ordinary people living in extraordinary times, following their journey through the mud of the trenches in France, through Palestine and Egypt, and a wood where they fight together to save our country from a common enemy, believing it to be a war to end all wars.

- *'Pandora's Box',* Amazon Kindle, 2011

- *Stone Cold Dead, a Thriller,* FeedARead.com, 2012

  A Bomber's Moon ... perfect conditions for a clandestine operation. And yet not everything is what it seems. Something is wrong. Too late the pilot realises the problem.

  Sixty-five years on Joe Maddison steps into a new day ... and into the perfect nightmare. As he struggles to understand what is happening, life as he knows it does a tail-spin out of control.

Lightning Source UK Ltd.
Milton Keynes UK
UKHW010626100821
388609UK00001B/51